Unauth of the Britain's Got Talent Magicians

Copyright 2017, Steve Piers Independent Publishing

No part of this publication may be reproduced, stored in a retrieval system whatever the heck that means, or transmitted in any form or by any means, whether that's electronic, mechanical, photocopying, recording, taking a photo of the pages and printing them out at Max Spielmann and turning them into a mouse mat or a key ring or a mug or whatever, or otherwise, without written permission from the publisher. Don't stick it on a torrent site or swap it for cigarettes. If reading this on a Kindle, do not drop it in the bath.

Dedicated to Robert from Robert's World of Magic (that guy who gets trapped in the bag and cut out by Keith Chegwin, you know, it's like, on every magic clip show on TV all the time. Wonder if he gets royalties? Bet he's a millionaire by now.)

Contents

- **Notes and Introduction**
- **Magical Thinking**
- **Finding the Method**
- **The Methods Described in This Book**
- **An explanation of pre-show work and 'Dual Reality'**
- **The BGT Magician's methods, secrets and review:**
- Series 1 – 2007 - Doctor Gore
- Series 2 – 2008 – The Deans of Magic, Sauris Nandi, Visage
- Series 3 – 2009 - Merlin Cadogan
- Series 4 – 2010 - Stevie Starr
- Series 5 – 2011 - David and Karen
- Series 6 – 2012 - Brynolf and Ljung
- Series 7 – 2013 - James More, Stevie Pink
- Series 8 – 2014 - Darcy Oake
- Series 9 – 2015 - Chloe L. Crawford, Jamie Raven, Michael Late
- Series 10 – 2016 - Christian Lee, Richard Jones
- Series 11 – 2017 – Tanba, DNA, Issy Simpson, Josephine Lee, Matt Edwards, Niels Harder
- **Afterword – The Masked Magician**

Notes

This book is not endorsed, published or connected in any way with Britain's Got Talent, America's Got Talent, or any of the shows worldwide, Simon Cowell, his companies, or anyone involved in the creation and production of the shows discussed. This book is written for the purposes of review and education on magic, performance techniques and showmanship. Whilst I have every confidence of the accuracy of the information contained within, all theories and methods discussed cannot be verified to be factual, or confirmed to be the specific methods used. All references to actual shows and performances are considered fair-use. I'm happy to correct any errors in future editions. Contents of this book are the opinions of the author and may not be correct.

Do not attempt to recreate any of the dangerous magic featured – whilst you are unlikely to be hurt by performing a card trick, some of the content can be extremely dangerous and could result in injury and/or death.

Introduction

As a magician, watching Britain's Got Talent evolve over eleven series has been an education for me. Initially, magic was greeted with cries of derision from the judges and it appeared to be career suicide to go on these shows. Millions of people would see you get booed off stage, the judges would hit their buzzers and you'd be forever known as the guy from the TV that didn't get through. As a working magician and magic dealer, I have met many famous magicians in my time, and some of them have told me their TV talent show tales. From one magician who claims that he is contacted every year with a promise that he will get straight through to the semi-finals if he agrees to appear, to one of the best magicians I have ever met having his routine trimmed to about 10 seconds (and of course he was buzzed off stage, with Amanda Holden wearing a particular expression of disgust at the "cards from mouth" routine being performed), it seemed the sensible approach was to ignore the lure of television fame to pursue a career of relative anonymity.

In later series, everything changed. Simon Cowell, a long time vocal opponent of the cheesy, cruise-ship performance style so often favoured by magicians, suddenly revealed a different side to his persona by enjoying some of the more exciting magic acts. Magicians such as David Penn (series 5) performed large scale stage illusions with flair and made it through to the semi finals. They started to see success from their appearances on the show, and at the end of series ten, Richard Jones won the overall series with his magic.

Magicians are often seen as out of date and uninspiring by audiences who remember the height of magic's success on TV in the 1980s. The glittery costumes, glamorous assistants, disappearing doves, appearing rabbits and cutting people in half can still be seen in holiday resorts and working-men's-club entertainments. In reality, magic has evolved beyond recognition, and advancements in technology have made the most extraordinary magical apparatus possible. Magic dealers sell all sorts of gimmicked devices to allow the most extraordinary magical feats to be performed and it's exciting to see so much of the craft back on television. Performers such as Dynamo, Penn and Teller, Criss Angel and David Blaine have made magic cool, and the TV talent shows are finally getting behind this most wonderful of hobbies. Darcy Oake even made dove magic cool!

Working as a magician makes it difficult for me to watch a performance through the eyes of a non-magician, and it is fascinating to me to hear theories about how the tricks are performed. Having attended magic conventions where the theatre audience is made up entirely of magicians, I can confidently tell you that magicians are the worst audience to work to. Their eyes burn the performer, never following the magicians misdirection, always looking exactly where the magician hopes they would not, and having an understanding of what I like to call magical thinking. Magical thinking is knowing that the situation is not as it appears, and the presentation is the key to the routine. Magical thinking makes a trick bigger and better through showmanship and inventiveness.

Let's say a magician offers you a choice from a deck of cards, and then reads your mind to determine which one you picked. The mind reading element of the trick should be the focus of the audience's attention. The magician should spend the overwhelming majority of the routine demonstrating their psychic abilities to the audience. This approach draws all attention away from the fact that the performer is a magician and has simply forced a specific card, whilst creating the illusion of a free choice. The trick becomes a demonstration of mind reading, of psychic powers and the style of presentation is far better than the magical performers you've seen in the past. I have met many amateur magicians in my years that meticulously practice secret moves and techniques, sometimes for years, forgetting that the audience isn't going to see the secrets. Practising to fool a magician is fun, but the audience is looking for excitement, charisma, stage presence and above all, a good enjoyable show. The real audience of non-magicians doesn't burn you like a magician would, and it bothers me when I meet performers that have not worked on their character, their stage persona. The audience is there to see you, not to watch a technical display of hidden secret moves. Some of the best magicians I have ever seen have performed very simple (and among magicians, very basic and well known) routines, but added their own spin on the presentation. These are the magicians that own the stage, the audience loves them, and yes, they do tend to do very well on shows like Britain's Got Talent.

Watching BGT, I became fascinated by the logistics of performing a magic show to such a massive audience. Imagine the pressure on the performer. When tricks go wrong, as they sometimes do, how do you ad-lib and move on with an audience of that size?

When I perform my current magic act, it lasts just over an hour and it was rehearsed over a period of six months. Trapdoors got stuck, elastic bands broke, audience volunteers forgot the card they chose, and so on. It's impossible to predict every single eventuality that can cause a problem with the routine and some of my more complex methods had to be dropped to remove the risk of anything going wrong. When a trick fails midway through, the magician can try to cover it up with 'multiple-outs' where the intended effect is dropped and the magician works with what they have to salvage the routine and bring it to an ending without revealing the failure. How much easier it would be to perform a routine that simply cannot go wrong. With the reassurance that the mechanics of the trick are straightforward enough to guarantee success, the next stage in the design of the show is to dress up the simple effect and make it appear more complex.

This is the secret, I believe, to winning a TV talent show with magic. Keep the method simple, straightforward and impossible to get wrong. Work on your interaction with the audience, scripting the performance to make sure that the spectator does not forget their chosen card, stands in the correct position, thinks of the right number and so on. The secret and the trick is never the winner in and of itself. The performer uses the magic to create their act, and it's the performer that goes on to win.

An Example.

Here's a trick that's designed to be so simple that it cannot fail. I'll explain the process, then we'll dress up the performance to make the simple trick a million times bigger and better.

This trick uses 'multiple outs' in its conclusion and this makes it completely safe – there's no possibility that the trick can go wrong. It's also an effect that I make and sell in my magic shop. The magician removes three large playing cards from an envelope, and places them face up on the table. He hands a magic wand to the spectator who is asked to wave the wand over the three cards. Whenever they feel ready they should tap just one card with the wand. The spectator then turns over the card they chose. Printed on the back it says "you will choose this card".

On sale in my shop for only five pounds, this trick comes with a disclaimer – if you buy it, please try to remember how you felt during the performance. Keep in mind that you were fooled. I explain this because many people buy the trick after a demonstration, just because they want to know how it works. But if I ask them how *they* think it works they come up with theories that are complicated and often rely on chance, coincidence, luck, probability and sleight of hand. Like many magic tricks the explanation is simple, so simple in fact that it can be disappointing. The audience know that the card they turned over has "you will choose this card" printed on the back. Usually, the first thing they do is to turn over the two remaining cards and check there is nothing printed on each of them. There isn't of course (that would be too easy!) but the spectator never asks to look inside the envelope that the performer is still holding in their hands. This irrelevant detail is the key to the method. Inside the envelope is a piece of white card, printed with the message "You will choose the King of Clubs". The other seemingly irrelevant item in this trick is the wand. Why did the magician give a wand to the performer? Surely they could have just as easily pointed to the card they wanted to choose? Again, the spectator never looks too closely at the wand. If they did, they would see it has a message printed along the length, "You will pick the Two of Diamonds".

That's what we call a multiple out – three different endings to the trick. The spectator hasn't seen the trick before, so they make the assumption that I would have asked them to turn over the card, whichever they chose. That's not how it works. If they choose the King of Clubs, I'll continue the trick by asking them to look inside the envelope that I have been holding the whole time. If they choose the Two of Diamonds, I'll ask them to look at the wand they are holding. The spectator never queries the wand or the envelope if the outcome of the trick results in them turning over the card on the table. Likewise, if they are told to look at the wand, they are too busy being baffled by the message on the wand to start questioning why I have been holding the envelope all the way through the trick. It never fails. Every option is covered.

This is a perfect trick in my opinion. For a start, I've been performing this for years in my shop and the only people who have ever called me on it were people who have studied magic. No ordinary member of the public (I really don't like the term 'laypeople but I'll have to use it from time to time, sorry') has *ever* worked it out and I have sold many sets over the years as many people pay up just to find out the method. They can initially seem disappointed in the simplicity of the secret, but then of course they take their new trick home, and bamboozle their friends with it.

I wanted to explain this trick at the beginning of my book, because it sets the tone for what's to follow.

Showmanship.

It's important that in demonstrating this trick I create a performance. It's easy to say "Choose a card", then "OK, look at the wand" and the trick would last about thirty seconds. In this way the trick is presented as nothing more than a fun little puzzle to be solved, but it's not magic. We need to make this trick bigger through the presentation. I'll do this by talking to the spectator and setting the scene whilst I lay out the cards on the table. I'll shift the focus away from the cards themselves and instead I will tell the spectator that I want to perform an experiment that will teach them about the way in which our free choices can be manipulated by suggestion and clever use of language. We're going to learn something about how the brain works.

"It's puzzling, but it means that you can convince people that you know things about them, predict ways people will behave, even to the point where you can make people do what you want them to do. I'll show you something really simple. I've got three playing cards here, and I want you to choose one of them. Don't choose it yet, because I want you to really think about it. You can see we have two picture cards and one number card. Perhaps you think I want you to choose the number card because the other two are more elaborate so it stands out as different. Or maybe, that's a ruse to make you ignore the number card, and I want you to concentrate on one of the two remaining picture cards. Now, I can see from the way you are holding your handbag that you are right handed, so If I wanted you to pick a specific card perhaps I would lay that out on the right? The important point here is I really want you to think *about your choice. I want you to know it's a completely free choice."*

After the card has been selected, we take a moment to ask why they chose that card, because the reveal of the prediction message signifies the end of the trick. The choice has now been made and this offers me a moment of down-time as the spectator's job is done and they can relax. I can take this opportunity to casually take back the wand or put down the envelope, depending on which card was chosen. This whole approach makes the performance more than simple coincidence or trickery; it becomes a demonstration of psychology and mind control.

Creating a bigger effect from a smaller routine is the key to success on a TV talent show, especially when the semi-final and final are live in front of an audience of millions. Imagine performing a mechanical trick where the mechanism breaks at the key moment. In your own live magic show, you can have alternate paths, different endings, a little bit of winging it, and ultimately get yourself out of a difficult situation. On TV, with only a couple of minutes to put your entire act across, you'd be absolutely destroyed if it went wrong. The acronym KISS, (Keep It Simple, Stupid!) is perfect here. Keep the mechanics to a minimum and keep the magic as self working as possible, then remember you are an entertainer, and your first job is to entertain!

Our example trick above is perfect – nothing can be allowed to go wrong in a performance and nothing can go wrong with this trick as every option is covered. The worst thing a magician can hear after asking the spectator "Was that the card you were thinking of?" is "Sorry, I can't remember!", and on live television this cannot be allowed to happen. This means that the methods being used must be bombproof. And the easy way to do that is to keep it simple!

I realise this book will not be for everyone, nor is it supposed to be. Just as buying a Jamie Oliver cook book won't give you the *talent* of a world class chef, knowing the methods of the Britain's Got Talent magicians risks reducing the content into puzzle solving. We know that a magician does not really saw a woman in half. We suspend our disbelief and enjoy the show. If I tell you there's a trick method involved, have I really told you anything you didn't know?

So who is this book aimed at? I hope that people who read this book are people with a desire to learn showmanship, and people who are interested in the art of magic, looking for a way in to learning the craft for themselves. In understanding the methods used, I believe it becomes obvious what a significant part showmanship and presentation have to play to make the trick into a performance. I want up and coming amateur magicians to stop obsessively practicing highly technical moves and techniques, to come out from the bedroom or magic club and work on their personality and performance. Work on being natural, funny and entertaining. Stop learning yet another way to locate a spectator's card in the pack and come up with a new and exciting way to entertain the audience using your own style to make that audience love you.

As I write this, the magic scene in theatre and on television has come back into favour. For the kids, CBBC's 'Help! My Supply Teacher is Magic' combines big illusions with simple tricks you can learn at home. Dynamo has filmed the last episodes of his Magician Impossible series and is touring theatres for the first time. Derren Brown has taken his incredible live shows to America and is wowing audiences for the first time in that country. There's never been a better time to see magic, to be inspired by magic and to get involved. If you feel you would like to become a magician, research magic books, join your local club, learn some methods but please remember the most important thing. The audience isn't there to see trickery or be tricked. The audience comes to see *you*. You are the performer, the entertainer. Sure, you can do these feats of magic, but *you* are at the heart of what they see and it's *you* that takes a magic show and turns it into a world class performance.

Magical Thinking.

The common personality trait I see in the most successful magicians is the ability to think magically. This is when a performer takes their well-honed skills and ideas and converts them into something that is real magic in the mind of the spectator. Magical thinking is especially important when keeping the method simple. Magical thinking turns the mundane into the miracle and places the focus on the presentation of magic, not the performance of a trick.

Many of the top magicians reveal their methods in print and on video, and these are often sold through magic dealers and conventions. It is easy to watch a performance and learn the routine, but it is also easy to fall into the trap of simply impersonating the performer rather than using the knowledge shared to help craft your own style. Many magicians prefer to learn from books for this reason. Books present the ideas and methods but without seeing the performance in action you are left to come up with the presentation yourself. The process of learning from a DVD easily becomes a lesson in mimicking the magician rather than learning. This is one of the reasons that I do not recommend trying to learn magic from YouTube videos on the internet, as so many of these clips feature badly performed tricks that rely on the reveal of the secret for their popularity. The learning objective for a magician is in taking the secret method and adapting it into a performance that allows them to express their own personality. Magical thinking is the key to this.

Magical thinking is the difference between simply performing a trick and totally mesmerising an audience that promotes a magician from mere entertainer to TV talent show winner. To understand this, the performer needs to be able to see the routine through the eyes of the audience, and present the magic as if from their point of view. Let's imagine that you have a coin on the table in front of you, and a spectator sitting opposite. You place your flat hand over the coin, and slide it towards you, making a fist which you lift into the air, the coin firmly concealed inside. What the spectator does not realise is that the coin never entered the fist, and in the motion of picking it up the coin was actually slid off the edge of the table into the magicians lap. This is a very basic trick, page one of the oldest books, and yet you'd be surprised how convincing this looks. You can now open your fist to reveal the coin has vanished. It's a simple trick, and it's been performed in the most basic way, and the only skill required was to convincingly look like you picked up the coin, instead of slipping it onto your lap. The problem here is the spectator will immediately start to think back about what they just saw. The coin was on the table, the magician picked it up and the coin was gone. Therefore the coin must have vanished during the pick-up. Simple. The magic wasn't magic, it was merely a puzzle to be solved.

Now, let's do the same trick again but this time we will add some magical thinking.

We sit at the table in the same way as the last example. We welcome the spectator and ask their name. We ask them if they ever feel like something they cannot explain has happened to them. These can be the most mundane examples, but they happen to all of us. When you put down your keys, and they just vanish. When you do DIY and drop a screw onto the floor it just disappears. It's strange isn't it?

Now we take the coin and add some relevance to the discussion by explaining why there is a coin on the table. We use an old style British Penny or a Silver Dollar to make the presentation a little more memorable. We make up a story as to why we have this in our possession. We talk about how our grandparents gave us this coin and showed us how money behaves unusually, just like when you lose your keys, you lose coins down the back of the couch. You make the trick about the discussion, not about the coin. We ask the spectator to sign their name on the coin.

In doing so, you casually pick up the coin, again dropping it into your lap, but now the focus is on you and your presentation. Instead of holding up a tightly screwed fist you hold your hand open with the backs of your fingers towards the spectator. Your thumb is behind the fingers, pretending to hold the coin in place. You pretend to pass the coin to your other hand as you take a handkerchief from your top pocket. You lay the handkerchief over the hand, and with a simple flick of the handkerchief reveal the coin has disappeared.

There are multiple ways this simple trick benefits from our magical thinking. Most significantly the flick of the handkerchief provides a moment of magic. In the eyes of the spectator this is the moment that the coin vanished. They may not know how you did it, but when they think back you have a multitude of magical moments that they may call you on. When you passed the coin from one hand to the other, did you really do that? Or perhaps you dumped the coin in the top pocket when you took out the handkerchief. Or perhaps the coin is hidden inside the handkerchief. The magical thinking in our routine has taken the special move that occurred as the coin was picked up from the table and obliterated it from the spectator's memory. They see the other things you may have done, but you can disprove all these things. The coin has vanished, the spectator doesn't know how you did it and all their explanations are disproved immediately. Meanwhile, they shared a memorable experience with you, enjoyed the atmosphere you created with the dialogue, and the whole routine was a two way interaction with a small magical happening at the end. Previously, all we had presented was a simple puzzle to be solved. To finish, our spectator, who has seen our hands empty since the routine ended, is invited to go back to the audience. As she stands up, the magician also stands, casually moving his chair back a little to allow him the room. In this normal looking movement the coin is reloaded back into the hand and held secretly. The magician shakes hands with the spectator and thanks them for their help. He then keeps hold of the hand and creates another moment of magic. Did you feel that? Did you see what just happened? The spectator looks into her hand and the signed coin is there. Beautiful.

A big trick doesn't need a big secret. It needs an entertainer, a performer, and a mindset to make a special experience for your volunteer.

Finding the Method.

To understand the logic of how a trick works, we need to look at the facts of the performance and focus on the truth of what we have seen, ignoring the parts where your brain fills in the gaps. As a magician, I hear spectators and volunteers discussing the trick they just saw with friends later and they often describe seeing something that simply didn't happen. The magic takes place in the minds of the audience, and it's easy to think that we saw something that didn't really happen. When we see the magician pass an object from one hand to the other we assume all is above board, but there's every chance that the magician performed the appropriate gestures whilst stealing the object away or retaining it in the same hand. The smallest movement can mask the biggest secrets.

TV magic is often difficult to work out because the director and magician will create the performance together ensuring that the camera follows the ideal audience viewpoint. The direction of the show mimics the misdirection intended by the performer. The live performance of magic is the only real opportunity to see magic unfiltered. Even whilst claiming there are no camera tricks used, an audience reaction shot can be inserted to ensure the home viewer cannot freeze frame and rewind to see the secret moves.

As you will learn when we examine eleven series worth of magicians later in this book, a number of clever moves and secret moments are not shown on screen and this can create a real miracle that cannot be explained. For example, the magician Jamie Raven performs a trick in series nine called Cardtoon. This is a great card trick and as we will learn the method requires moving a chosen card to the bottom of the deck. When this trick was performed on Britain's Got Talent the deck was not touched during the performance. This means that either the card that was selected by the judge was already on the bottom of the deck (there's a one in 52 chance of that through pure luck) or the crafty move was edited out to make the broadcast flow better.

Having said that, there is a key thought process that can be a great help when working out any magical methodology. For example, if a magician hands you a book and reads your mind to tell you the word you were looking at then could they do the trick without the book? Why should you have to select a playing card from the deck at random when you could just think of a card? Looking at the magician's props on stage we wonder, if this performer really could make his assistant disappear using magic, why does he need to put her in the big box? Why does he obscure her with a curtain? The key to the trick can lie in the most mundane of places. I perform a very difficult mathematics based trick and under the hot stage lights I am prone to forgetting the formula, so I write the formula on a sticky label and attach it to my marker pen. This way I can glimpse at the information I need whilst looking like I'm naturally writing on the whiteboard. The astute audience member might wonder, why doesn't he just shout out the answer, why does he need to write it out? But I need my pen, the secret is in the pen. If the magician has an elaborate prop, or even a common or garden prop, could that be the key to the illusion and could the magician perform without it?

To understand the mindset required in working out a method, I'd like to use a card trick that was shown to me by my grandfather when I was very young. He presented the trick to me and challenged me to work it out. It took a while, but I managed by focussing on what we did know to be true, and puzzling out the rest. I present this to you now so you may try to work it out as well.

Take a deck of cards and remove any nine cards (no jokers). Mix them up and place three piles of cards on the table, with three cards in each pile. Now play the role of the spectator and choose one of the piles. Lift a pile and turn it over to reveal the bottom card. Remember this card.

Now take all three piles and put them back together to make one pile of nine cards. In doing so, make sure the pile you chose first ends up on top, which will make your chosen card the third from the top in the pile. Now, we will explain to the audience that we are going to perform a spelling trick.

"Magic! M.A.G.I.C, this is going to be magic. Are you ready?"

Now deal the cards onto the table one at a time, spelling the value of the card. For example, if the card was a seven, you would deal S.E.V.E.N, dealing one card for each letter. When you have done this put the remaining pile from your hand on top of the pile on the table. Pick up the complete pile from the table and repeat, this time spelling O.F, dealing two cards. Then again place the remaining cards in your hand on top of the pile on the table, pick up the whole lot, and deal the suit. For example H.E.A.R.T.S, deals five cards one at a time. Put the rest of the cards in your hand on top, pick it all up, and tell the audience that you promised them some real magic, and then spell out M.A.G.I.C. Turn over the card on "C" and it will be their chosen card. How on earth can that possibly be?

Let's now look at the facts of the performance to work out the method.

First of all, the trick just worked, there were no funny moves and no sleights of hand used. The only thing the performer needed to remember was to ensure the chosen card was third from the top when the nine card deck was reassembled. A good way to begin puzzling this out is to turn the chosen card face up so we can easily see where the card is in the deck at any time. For this example, let us pretend you have picked the ace of clubs and this is now in the third position from the top.

The first thing you will do is deal three cards onto the table, (A, C, E). This reverses the order of those three cards. Then you place the remaining cards on top. We are now left with a situation where the top three cards have been reversed, but the remaining cards were not. Your chosen card is now three from the bottom of the deck.

The next thing to do is to pick up the pile and deal the top two cards onto the table (O,F), and then drop the rest of the pack on top. Again, this reverses the order of the two cards, but does not change the order of those that were not dealt. Your card is now 5th from the top.

Finally the cards are picked up again and we deal five cards (C.L.U.B.S). Your card will still be 5th from the top. This means when we deal M.A.G.I.C it will be your card.

But how can this trick work? What we do know is that the trick can be performed with a regular deck of cards. We know any nine cards can be chosen. We know that when we copy the magician's performance the routine still works. And we know the trick works with any card chosen. So let's go back and play with this until we work out the magic behind the effect.

In stage one of the trick when we spelled ACE, we dealt three cards onto the table and our card ended up third from the bottom. If we spelled TWO, the order of the cards would have been the same. SIX or TEN also leaves the deck in the same position. Spelling any value will involve dealing at least 3 cards (to spell ACE, ONE, TWO, SIX, TEN), 4 cards (spelling FOUR, FIVE, NINE), 5 cards (THREE or EIGHT) or 6 cards (to spell SEVEN). The value of card you spell will only disturb the order of the cards above your chosen card which does not affect the trick because your card will always remain third from the bottom. No numbers have less than three letters when spelled out, JACK, QUEEN and KING also fulfil the requirement so your chosen card will always end in the same position in the deck.

Step two is always the same as you always spell the same word, "OF", leaving your card in the fifth position.

Step 3 is again just more of the same because as long as the word you spell has 5 or more letters, you will only be disturbing the order of the cards above your card in the deck and your card will always be fifth from the top at the end. Whether you spell CLUBS, HEARTS, SPADES or DIAMONDS does not matter, as each of those options has enough letters. This means that when you spell MAGIC, the C will always be the chosen card.

By experimenting with different spellings and keeping watch on the position of the chosen card it is easy to see how it works. By focussing on what we know to be factual, ignoring the magicians patter about his apparent powers, we concentrate on what we can see and solve the puzzle.

But, why should we stop there now we know one method? The secret is just the beginning, and we can improve this trick with a little magical thinking. For example, if we know the name of the spectator, how many letters are in their name? Can we spell their name instead of MAGIC at the end? If their name is Steven, can we call them Steve? Can we use a personal five letter word for the last stage of the trick? Instead of spelling magic, we can spell to something more personal. How about spelling "David is amazing" instead of seven of clubs? That becomes a bigger mind-bender. A simple trick goes a long way when combined with amazing presentation and magical thinking, and the further away you get from the facts of the performance, the harder it becomes to work out the method.

The Methods Revealed in this Book

In my work as a magician and magic dealer, I attend conventions and shows where magic apparatus is sold. Magic methods are discussed openly, and the most ordinary looking objects are given magical powers. From the classics of literature (William Shakespeare, Sherlock Holmes, Dracula), magicians produce ordinary looking books that have been rewritten to allow a magician to know exactly which word you have chosen. Or how about the clipboard and pen that looks like it cost a pound at Office Max, yet uses Bluetooth to transmit whatever you draw to the mind reader's own iPad? A visit to a magic dealer is fascinating, even to a non-magician.

During the FISM International World Championships of Magic in 2012, I saw 150 performers over seven days, showing off their stage acts in the hope of winning the competition. One act started his performance by walking onto the stage wearing a top hat and tails. He made doves appear apparently from nowhere. Each time a new dove appeared he walked over to an ornate wooden table and placed the bird on a perch. By the end of the act there must have been ten birds on the perch. For his finale, he walked over to the birds, covered them with a silk cloth, whipped the cover away and the birds had disappeared. The trick was impressive and I enjoyed the performance. Later in the day another magician started their performance by walking onto the stage towards a table, suspiciously looking like this was the exact same table. Of course this probably means that both magicians had bought the same magic gimmicked table, maybe even from the same dealer. An experienced magician begins to recognise certain props and this tells me that this magician is going to perform dove magic, before he's even begun the act. I don't know the exact make and model of the table, but I've seen four magicians using it since then, and every time the magician places birds on a perch, then they disappear. I can say with absolute certainty that this table is the key to the routine as it's too much of a coincidence that all the dove magicians I saw use it. The prop table must have some mechanism that allows the doves to be quickly concealed inside. The more magicians I see performing, the more I come to recognise the props.

Does this mean the magicians were absolutely without question using this method? No, we cannot prove anything. Is it extremely likely that the table is a specific prop for making doves vanish? Yes, it surely has to be. It's too much of a coincidence that all the dove magicians happened to purchase the same table because it looks nice – it's a special dove table.

Should a magician on Britain's Got Talent pull out a book of The Complete Works of Shakespeare, do I assume this to be just a regular book from a bookstore? The audience does. But when I know that I have seen a book that looks exactly like the one he is using for sale at a Magic Convention, where the book is specially manufactured to allow exactly that same effect to be performed, does that mean I know the method? No, I cannot prove that. But it is likely that he's using the trick book? Yes, I think so.

So, I won't be possible for me to say these methods are absolutely without question the methods used on stage by the Britain's Got Talent magicians. These methods that follow are the methods I would use if I wanted to perform the same effect. However, I have the confidence that these are the methods used from my educated standpoint of being a magician and magic dealer, and if they are not entirely correct I believe the correct method will be similar.

An explanation of pre-show work and 'Dual Reality'

Pre-show work and Dual Reality are amazing tools for a magician to use in a live environment. Pre-show work involves asking a volunteer if they would like to take part in the show as a volunteer, usually as the audience are entering the theatre and finding their seats. The magician has a conversation that will involve what they will see in the show. They may ask the volunteer if they have a favourite name, for example. They will ask what it is, and explain that it's great that they have a favourite name because one of the tricks they will see later involves favourite names. The magician will tell the volunteer that later during the show, we'll use you as a volunteer in one of the tricks. The magician uses this volunteer in the show and among the mind reading effects they are asked to write their favourite name. Seeing as the audience do no not know about the pre-show conversation the reveal of the name looks like true mind reading.

Dual Reality involves the magician performing a trick to a spectator on stage. The spectator is not a stooge and is not in on the trick. Through use of language and the audience's perception of events, two tricks are performed simultaneously, with a major effect and a minor effect. The spectator on stage takes part in a routine and sees the events that take place from their own point of view. They forget that the audience has their own perspective on the show and don't realise that the audience is seeing something that appears much bigger and more impressive than the actual events happening. For example, the volunteer may be asked to choose a word. The audience believes that the volunteer could pick any word from the English language, because they cannot see that there is a list of five words for the volunteer to choose from. The list is in plain sight of the volunteer who understands the vague wording of "choose any word" to mean "choose any word from this list of five". At the end of the routine the mind reader knows the word that the volunteer is thinking of, and the volunteer is impressed that the mind reader could know what word was chosen. The audience saw a much bigger effect because they believe that the volunteer could have thought of any totally random word. Dual Reality effects can sometimes be spotted by noting the disparity between the audience's big reaction and the volunteer's more subdued response.

An excellent example of Dual Reality involves a mind reader predicting images drawn by volunteers on stage. Volunteers were invited to draw a picture each on large pads. Each of the audience members was instructed to imagine their picture in a bright colourful image in their minds, then they could draw their images on the pads. The audience at this point think the volunteers can be drawing anything they choose, but they do not realise that on each paper, written in light pencil to prevent the audience seeing it, there is already an instruction to the artist regarding their image. This could say "You are player one, your image is a TREE." The next card could say "You are player 2, your image is a FISH". The language used by the magician refers to the images as "your image" and the spectator sees nothing unusual about this because they do not know what the end result of the trick is going to be. They simply follow the instructions they are given. The drawings are placed in envelopes, which are again secretly marked so the performer can tell which envelope contains which image. As the climactic moment to the performance arrives the magician uses all his acting skills to suggest that he his using his mind powers to determine the contents of the first envelope. He explains his thought processes:

"I'm getting the sensation of an image created by someone with a great sense of fun in their lives. I think this is someone who has a number of important decisions to be made at the moment, and someone who is looking to travel soon. The way they have

drawn the image tells me they feel they should be more organised in their life. I think this image was drawn by our volunteer Amanda, and this is a picture of a... tree! "

The envelope is dramatically opened and revealed to show the image was indeed drawn by the named volunteer and was indeed a tree. This is repeated for each volunteer. They all believe that the trick has been a success as the magician knew it was their picture, even though it was sealed in an envelope. Also the cold-reading statements (statements that apply to everyone – the examples I used above would pretty much apply to anyone in the demographic of that volunteer) add further distraction to the overall method. Each volunteer saw one main miracle, which was that the magician knew which envelope contained their image.

The audience however saw a much bigger picture. They cannot understand how the magician knew what was inside the envelope, which volunteer drew the image that was in there and what the image would be. The audience don't know that the volunteers were instructed to draw specific things, and as far as they are concerned the three of them had a free choice to draw anything in the world that they wanted to.

Dual reality can be combined with pre-show work with unbelievable results. In our example, the magician could ask the audience member to draw a picture, and write their favourite name underneath the drawing. Then the magician can reveal an envelope that was clearly in view on stage the whole time, and open it up to reveal his 'prediction' of a picture of a house with the name written underneath.

Pre-show work is an incredible tool for the mentalism performer and can be used to dazzling effect in the right environment. However, in the TV Talent show, it would be impractical to use pre-show work, especially when impressing the judges. Simon Cowell seems to me to be the sort of judge who would call the magician on the technique during the judge's comments. Having said that, the beauty of dual reality is that the spectators involved do not realise the deception, and these techniques work well in a live environment.

Enough explanation – that's my pre-show work done, and let's move on to the main event. The following is a breakdown, critical analysis and explanation of all eleven years of magic in Britain's Got Talent. I hope the information gives you a better understanding of magic, performance and showmanship. Who knows, maybe you could be a winner in the next series?

Series 1 – 2007

Doctor Gore

www.youtube.com/watch?v=WPBnpsHN4_4

Semi Finalist Roger, aka Doctor Gore arrived on stage with two assistants and wearing a white laboratory coat splattered with blood! He auditioned with an act called Madness and Magic, which looked like it was heavily edited for television. After detonating a blood filled squib on one assistants face (for reasons that were unclear in the TV broadcast), Doctor Gore threatened the audience with an electric saw, shouting, "Do you want some?"

Doctor Gore lay one of his assistants onto the table and used a wooden piece of apparatus to attach her in place. Unable to move, the assistant could do nothing but lie there and scream while the Doctor slid the blade of the power saw into the wooden frame. The blade cut all the way across, apparently slicing the poor girl straight across the stomach. As the wooden frame was removed, she jumped straight up off the table and appeared completely unharmed.

The method for this trick dates back many years, and was originally built by Jack Hughes, a magician famous for his invention and design of large scale stage apparatus. The wooden frame forms a bridge shape that fits over the assistant's stomach. The saw blade is inserted into the left side of the archway, and as the saw is moved across the frame the blade detaches from the handle. The empty saw handle is slid across the top of the frame, creating the illusion that the blade is still attached and slicing through the assistant. When the handle reaches the opposite side of the archway it slides onto a duplicate blade hidden in the frame. This allows the saw to be lifted out of the frame with the blade still clearly visible, and creates an impressive looking illusion that the blade remained attached to the handle throughout the performance and passed through the assistant. Now, you know there are two blades and the first disconnects when inserted into the wooden frame, and the second one connects to the saw on the other side of the frame. Simple, but what a great performance!

This violent and gory approach worked and the judges loved it. Doctor Gore later said he expected to be crucified, but even Simon Cowell, who up to this point had made no secret of his hatred of magicians, gave a yes to the performance, and Doctor Gore sailed through to the Semi Finals. Unfortunately he was buzzed off stage by all three judges in the semi, and did not get to complete his performance.

Doctor Gore was the only magician in the first series of Britain's Got Talent, and it was a shame that he did not get to complete his act in the semi final. However, there were a number of complaints to the TV regulator Ofcom about the audition and in my opinion it was quite strong content for a family show. I wondered if the judges may have buzzed Doctor Gore off stage so quickly in the semi finals to avoid any further complaints!

Series 2 – 2008

Sauris Nandi

www.youtube.com/watch?v=M1CeBTGkudU

A very traditional magical routine with a smattering of Indian atmosphere and music, Sauris' performance fell flat with the audience and the judges, with Simon buzzing at the point of the big reveal. Simon judged the performance with a discussion that pretty much explained the secret and there's not a great deal more I can add to the explanation. In fact, between Piers Morgan insinuating, "That is the same girl, right?" and Simon bringing the audience's attention to the platform that the magician had used throughout the performance, the act was almost completely explained away on the night.

Sauris arrived on stage in full Indian dress and showed the judges a large basket. He showed the inside of the basket and lifted it in the air to demonstrate that it was empty. He placed the basket on the aforementioned platform and covered it with a black blanket. Then, as expected in this kind of trick, the blanket started to lift and it was clear that someone or something was standing up inside the basket. Sauris removed the blanket and sure enough there was a beautiful assistant wearing a shiny yellow, revealing costume. The blanket was placed back over her head, and a few moments later Sauris whisked it away to show she had disappeared. Then, just seconds later the assistant could be seen at the other end of the studio, striking a pose to accept her applause, which came from an apparently underwhelmed audience.

Simon's comments about the platform were bang on the money, and the bulk of the trick hinges on the basket and platform being one magical prop with both elements designed to work together. The platform looks thin, but this is an optical illusion. Many large scale pieces of magic apparatus are wheeled out onto the stage on platforms and tables, but close inspection shows that the table is part of the trick. The most famous of these is the traditional sword-box, where an assistant is placed inside a wooden box and many swords are stabbed through each side until it appears there is no-where that the assistant could be. The reality is that the box is not resting on the table but is attached to it. From the outside the box looks like it is standing on the table but from the inside the box is considerably taller than it would appear, and there is plenty of space in the bottom of the box which is inside the thickness of the table itself.

A similar approach is being taken with Sauris' basket, with the girl being hidden inside the platform. The platforms are often painted with a black outline and bright, reflective stripes to mask the real thickness, and although it appears that the assistant could not fit inside, there is enough space, often for more than one assistant. When I first saw Sauris' routine, I imagined the girl would magically change to another girl – there certainly appears to be enough room in the platform to allow that to happen, although this doubles the wages bill of the magician! The platform usually has a hidden door which can be pushed upwards into the inside of the basket. The bottom of the basket will be hinged in the same way so the girl can climb out of the platform into the basket. She then slowly stands up under the blanket, until the magician removes it to reveal the mysterious, magical girl that appeared from apparently thin-air!

As the assistant is re-covered by the blanket, you can see that the blanket is hanging from a thread, invisible to the TV camera. The girl simply drops back into the basket, and into the hidden area in the platform. A concealed shell is sewn into the blanket directly underneath the thread. This shell is the same shape as the top of the assistant's head, so when she ducks down into the platform the blanket remains undisturbed and it looks like she is still standing.

As Sauris whisks the blanket away one last time, we see the assistant has disappeared, and immediately reappeared at the rear of the audience. This is a common trope in stage magic, with the assistant often blowing a whistle to attract the audience's attention. There are many stage illusions that allow the performer to escape secretly from the stage so they can reappear elsewhere. I read of one magician many years ago that had a trapdoor in the stage, and a purpose built system of ladders and trampolines within the wall and ceiling cavity, allowing him to disappear from the stage and reappear above the audience, standing on a chandelier. I've seen assistants sneaking back into the theatre and hiding in position ready to reveal their location to the audience whilst I was supposed to believe she was still in a box that was slowly being suspended in the air. For Sauris' performance there is an extra complication in that there is no time between the last time we saw the assistant on stage and the moment we see her so far away. Even without the magical showmanship that would be required to sneak her off stage, it would take longer than this to run to the back of the audience. However, Piers Morgan seems spot on in his opinion when he asks, "Is that the same girl?"

Magicians often use twins in their act. This offers many advantages to the working magician. They can use an assistant throughout their show building the illusion that there is only one assistant. Then, they can perform the switch as needed, making their assistant disappear and reappear in seconds. I spoke to one magician who told me that his act involved himself and one assistant performing for the audience for 45 minutes, whilst the twin was hidden inside a table for the entire routine. The magician wowed his audience with a spectacular finale as the assistant disappeared from the stage and instantly jumped up out of the table behind the audience, but I couldn't help feeling sorry for the assistant that had to hide for so long, every night of the summer season. To add insult to injury, as this was the final effect of the show, the assistant that worked so hard throughout the show wouldn't be able to take a bow and receive their applause because as far as the audience were concerned the girl they were applauding was the girl they had been watching all night.

Sauris didn't go further in the competition.

Visage

www.youtube.com/watch?v=tk7KBETHf8U

The quick change act is another of the magic 'standards' and has featured on the international "Got Talent" shows by various performers. The leaders in this field (in my opinion) are David and Dania, who not only wrote the book on quick change (literally, they sell it at magic conventions), but also do the most incredible lectures explaining the techniques, many of which they invented themselves. David and Dania appeared on America's Got Talent, and absolutely stole the show, Visage come a distant second in my view and their live vocals during the quick change seem to me to be an unnecessary addition, adding a layer of cheese to an otherwise interesting performance.

The sword box technique, described earlier as part of the Sauris Nandi explanation is used here to provide a surprise opening to the performance. At the side of the stage, an ordinary looking cardboard box stands on a suspiciously thick table. The side of the table surface has a silver stripe across the centre of the thickness of the table, disguising the black stripes both above and below the silver one. This conceals the thickness of the table which is deep enough to hide the performer inside. The male performer shows there is nothing in the cardboard box, the box is replaced on the table, the performer opens the secret hatch on the table surface and scrambles out ready for the box to be removed, revealing the lady and commencing the performance. It is worth noting that when an act is performed to music like this it provides cues so the hidden lady can know exactly the correct time to stand, knowing that the magician will replace the cardboard box at exactly the moment before she would be seen climbing out of the table.

The quick change act, when performed well, is an incredible sight to behold. Each performer will use their own methods, but it usually involves the artiste beginning the act wearing many layers of clothes, specifically designed for the purpose of quick change. These clothes are made from the thinnest and lightest materials available, and it can be a challenge for the performer to act as if they are wearing just one outfit as the weight of so many layers really adds up! It is difficult for this kind of performance to take place without perfect arrangement and scheduling because the artiste must prepare themselves with all the costumes just minutes before going on stage. Should the performance be delayed, the performer would need to take off the clothing due to the weight and the heat of wearing so many layers at once.

In addition to the thin materials, dresses are often designed to appear skimpier than they really are, with flesh coloured materials creating the illusion of plunging necklines and short sleeves that look convincing to an audience. This allows a smaller layer to be removed to show a fuller looking costume. The audience believes that the new dress could not have been concealed below the previous one and this sells the illusion that the performer is getting changed behind the curtain.

Press-studs are often used to hold the front of the dress to the back, and the performer can be seen to strike a pose just before the change, with their hands where the press-studs are. As soon as the curtain is lifted the layer is ripped away and falls to the floor. The curtain conceals the layer of the dress that drops to the floor, and it can be seen that the magician is careful to drop the curtain on stage with a small fold to conceal any parts of the dress that stay on the floor.

Other secrets involve use of a curtain that does not reach the floor but is held in the air by the magician. The costume layer is still removed, but the layer is dropped into a pocket on the back of the curtain as the artiste passes behind it.

Another technique that is used by quick change artists is to design a dress where the top half is held in place with press-studs, but when released the top half unfolds and becomes the bottom half of the next layer. This technique allows the performer to mask the change in more interesting ways that the traditional curtain, because this method does not require a layer to be concealed on the floor. The best use of this method involves going from a short skirt to a long flowing dress. The dress is concealed as the bust of the performer who appears to be wearing something small, then released to form the bottom half of a long flowing dress, without leaving a layer on the floor that would have needed to be disguised from the audience's view by a curtain.

The key to a good quick change routine is to perform a combination of these techniques, so just as the audience thinks they know what's going on, a short dress turns to a long dress, or a transformation takes place without the curtain. By continually switching techniques the audience is dumbfounded by the magic on display.

The three judges buzzed Visage off in the semi final, with criticism of the singing from the judges. Piers Morgan called the performance "complete professional suicide" which is completely unfair as the quick change element was performed skilfully and well. To my mind, Piers Morgan was often just plain rude and not constructive in his criticism and I am glad he was replaced by David Walliams in the later series. If you don't know the secrets the singing may have been cheesy but singing whilst smoothly performing the quick-changes is incredibly hard to do, and I felt that the judges were unfair on Visage.

The Deans of Magic

www.youtube.com/watch?v=PrKXqPO0ilY

Along with Visage, the Deans of Magic made it through to the semi finals, but neither got through to the final in 2008. The Deans did well to get as far as they did, with their audition receiving buzzes from Simon and Amanda. Amanda specifically mentioned their erotic dancing and sexy moves were unsuitable for the audience at home, but I couldn't help thinking that maybe it all looked a little too ridiculous rather than sexy. This married couple had been together for twenty years and it really showed. One judge commented that some things should stay behind closed doors and I am inclined to agree.

Similar to Sauris' act discussed earlier, The Deans audition involved flaming swords placed into a barrel with the woman inside. Obviously the sword does not pierce the assistant but either goes above or around her. The barrel can be placed on a table in the same way that Sauris used his platform, allowing the assistant to completely leave the box for ultimate safety.

In the semi final, the first buzz came immediately as a piece of special magician's string was set alight and magically changed into a necklace. The necklace is concealed in the hand holding the string from above. Flash string, as it is called, is treated with a chemical that makes it produce a huge flash as it burns. The string also evaporates so there is nothing left behind. Flash products that can be purchased by magicians also include flash wool, flash paper, flash playing cards, flash banknotes and so on. Also some manufacturers create solid objects that are made from the same materials such as flash candles. As the string creates the flash, the necklace is dropped from the hand above and the transformation from string to necklace is complete

The three judges buzzed at this early stage, with Piers Morgan describing the act as "one of the most boring things I have seen in my entire life" to rapturous applause from the crowd. However from my point of view as a magician I felt it was unfair to buzz so soon as there was a whole performance still to come, and some of the best magic performances I have seen start small and build to something incredible. By ending the act early we can only guess what was to come, and this was the last we saw of The Deans of Magic in Britain's Got Talent, and the end of all the magic in series two.

Series 3 – 2009

In a disappointing series for magic, there was a distinct lack of traditional magic in series three, with only one act remotely coming under this category. Merlin Cadogan, a holiday park entertainer made it to the semi finals with extraordinary demonstrations of escapology. Depending on the methods used to escape from the padlocks and chains that shackle the performer into place, escapology can come under the category of magic trick, with concealed secrets allowing the performer to get out whenever he needs. Other practitioners of this art do it for real, and a huge amount of skill is needed as there is a real threat that something could go wrong putting the Escapologist's life in jeopardy.

Merlin Cadogan

www.youtube.com/watch?v=q7ZnNPzEBU4

In the audition, Merlin wore a large diver's helmet and entered the stage with a tube in his mouth which poked out of the top, allowing him to breathe. His assistant wrapped him in chains and padlocked them tightly onto his body, then filled the helmet with water. Simon asked for the Merlin to confirm that everything was going correctly before the tube was removed.

Merlin then has the length of time he can hold his breath to get out of the chains, juggle three clubs that happen to be on fire, then get the helmet off before he drowns in the water.

In determining whether I believe the chain escape was genuine escapology or magic trickery we only have the evidence of the broadcast episode to make up our minds. Trickery can involve a pin slid between two links of the chain to create a small loop that is hidden from view. Removing the pin releases the loop which makes the whole chain looser and allows the magician to shake it to the floor. Other trick methods could involve break-away locks which look like real heavy duty padlocks but are gimmicked to allow the magician to easily unlock them when required. Alternatively, he could be using the skills that take years to learn in the field of Escapology. Books are available on the subject, teaching the skills needed to pick locks, create wriggle room and to exploit vulnerabilities in the way that a chain does not smoothly wrap around the magician. Small kinks can be used to gain leverage, a hand can be freed and this could be used to unpick the locks. This does require an enormous amount of study and uses a great deal of skill. In the TV broadcast the escapology went on behind a raised curtain and if this was a genuine piece of skilled escapology I would suggest it would be more exciting to watch without the curtain. Does this mean that this was a magic trick? It's impossible to say for sure.

Judging by his follow up act in the final which was definitely real escapology I can see how talented Merlin is, but in this performance the chain escape looked fake to me because of the need to cover the action with a curtain.

Upon freeing himself from the chains, Merlin juggled the fire clubs then freed himself from the diver's helmet and the water. This was a breathtaking performance, but in time he would create a much stronger routine for the Semi Final.

With the massive audience exposure of these shows, Merlin came up with a routine that was something the audience would remember for a long time. Tied into a strait-jacket, Merlin was lifted round ten feet from the group, suspended upside down whilst hanging from a thick rope. To add to the excitement the rope was set on fire! Merlin managed to escape from the straight-jacket and unhooked his feet, allowing him to lower himself to the safety of the ground.

For me, I enjoyed this performance, although as such a memorable routine I had a very clear recollection of the time I saw the same routine being performed better by one of my favourite magical performers, Shahid Malik. Shahid is an extremely talented showman and performer, and has shown incredible bravery (and some would say stupidity) by performing the most daring escapology I have ever seen. In fact, Shahid can be seen in the Channel 5 (UK) documentary "When Magic Goes Horribly Wrong", as he appears in the show a number of times telling of the times his magic has failed live on television. In the 1980s, during a performance on TV's Pebble Mill show, live on television at one o'clock in the afternoon Shahid did the same routine as described earlier, but outside, hanging from a crane some eighty feet in the air. As the rope was set on fire and Shahid was lifted into the air, he commenced the escape using similar technique to Merlin. Shahid wriggled and managed to free his arms, and escaped from the straight-jacket which dropped to the ground with a thud. Still hanging upside down, Shahid used his strength to lift himself towards his feet, and unhooked himself. Now the right way up, Shahid waved to the audience to show he was freed and their applause showed they were impressed with the performance. Then, unexpectedly and without rhyme or reason, Shahid let go of the rope and plunged to the ground. The TV broadcast didn't show his body as it landed on the ground with a bigger thud and the broadcast cut back to the studio and the show continued. Shahid was exceptionally lucky not to have been seriously injured by the fall, or even killed – and managed to join the broadcast from the studio later to explain to the concerned viewers that he was unhurt. It's an astonishing piece of footage, and unbelievable that Shahid fell so far unharmed.

Shahid Malik appeared a number of times on the "When Magic Goes Horribly Wrong" show, and each of the clips is a testament to the bravery and madness of this kind of work. In another clip, Shahid is tied to a post in the ground, surrounded by bales of hay which are set on fire and has no-time to escape. He emerges from the flames with his body alight and rolls on the floor in agony. He is immediately taken to hospital. His magical assistant (who is also his wife) participates in another of Shahid's famous routines when she climbs into a cardboard box which has swords thrust through it. The sword box is a traditional magic trick and the illusion costs thousands of pounds to buy, but Shahid's version uses wooden dowels and a cardboard box, with the dowels being slammed though with such energy it seems an incredibly violent way to do the trick, and his assistant has discussed the bruises and injuries she has sustained in the performance of this routine, including almost losing an eye. However, the danger and excitement, combined with excellent showmanship means Shahid Malik is a magician you would never forget and is highly respected by his peers.

Merlin's version of the suspended rope trick seems to be performed for real. I do not see any evidence of trick breakaway locks, and the straps look genuinely tied. The burning rope is a great demonstration of showmanship as the fire is above the performer and the heat of the flames rises, keeping the performer safe below. Also when lighter fuel is applied to a piece of rope, evaporation of the liquid occurs. When the rope is set alight the vapour of the fuel burns brightly but the rope itself does not. The rope is surrounded by a layer of fire burning in the air around it. Magicians use this knowledge to create spectacular illusions. My favourite application is the Fire Wallet. I have owned one of these wallets for twenty years and it has been on fire in my hands more time than I care to remember, but the wallet itself still looks great and undamaged. The wallet has a thick strip of gauze sewn inside in a section that is separate to the credit cards and other contents. Next to the gauze is a mechanism with a flint to create a spark, similar to what you'd find in a cigarette lighter. The gauze is soaked in lighter fluid, and when the magician opens the wallet they flick the lighter mechanism to make a spark and a miniature bonfire leaps out of the wallet. The fire can be extinguished by slamming the wallet closed. Using the same theory as the burning rope the gauze is still intact in the wallet, even after twenty years of use.

A popular theory on strait- jacket escapes comes into play when the performer's arms are tied behind their back. The arms are folded and buckles are tightened at the back of the jacket so the prisoner cannot move their arms and the buckles are out of reach. When the escapologist is placed into the jacket they can raise their arms forward as they are tied down, and this leaves a little extra space to wriggle. Instead of the arms being tightly tied against the chest, they are just that bit looser, but the magician mimes that the buckles are tight. During the escape, this extra wiggle room comes into play as the performer manages to get one arm over their head. From this point, it's a simpler job to get the whole jacket off and then just a demonstration of physical ability when the magician flips their body up to reach their feet. They remove their feet from the shackles and navigate their way out. This is a genuine feat of escapology and although easier than it may appear, it's definitely not something I would attempt, and I would not recommend anyone does this. Shahid Malik was lucky not to be killed when he fell so far, but even at a height of ten feet, a fall to the ground when hanging upside down could very easily be fatal. Even with tricks and magical props being used to facilitate an easy escape the trick would be incredibly dangerous, so Merlin deserves recognition for doing it for real.

Sadly there were no other magical performances in this series, and Merlin did not make it through to the final.

Series 4 – 2010

Stevie Starr

https://www.youtube.com/watch?v=ethCJ4bfJkg

In another disappointing year for magic fans, there was only one performer who could be described as a magician, and this guy is completely unique. Appearing on Czechoslovakia's Got Talent in 2011 and America's Got Talent in 2015, Stevie's skill has allowed him to travel the world, amazing and shocking audiences in equal measure. Stevie has discussed in interviews how he came to realise he could regurgitate items down his throat and back again, and there's no better explanation for this "trick" than to say that he's doing exactly what it looks like he's doing. At least, the regurgitation is real. Stevie has become famous for taking objects such as light bulbs, snooker balls and even goldfish, placing the items in his mouth and inhaling them down his throat, and regurgitating them at will. Whilst I believe this act to be genuine, I know that I would perform magic trick methods combined with this skill to create a bigger effect still, and I believe this is what Stevie did for his semi final audition.

Stevie asked Amanda Holden to give him a ring from her finger and Amanda said she only had her engagement ring. Amanda reluctantly handed it over and Stevie continued to perform a feat which I believe would be impossible, even with his regurgitating ability.

Before we discuss this further, I should share an anecdote I heard at a magic convention from a magician who was lecturing about precautions a performer can take in order to protect themselves from legal action when a trick goes wrong. He explained that he was using a prop known as a "Ring Wallet". This is an ordinary looking wallet that has metal loop hooks inside for holding keys. One of the loops is on an elastic reel and can be pulled away from the wallet and secreted in the hand. The magician can take a ring from a volunteer and secretly hook the metal loop over the ring whilst it is concealed from view by the hand. The wallet stays in the magician's back pocket and the thread of the reel is black and cannot be seen by the audience. The magician then shows the ring one last time then makes a magical gesture. The ring looks like it vanishes instantly, but in reality it has shot back into the wallet due to the tension of the elastic reel. The magician gets applause for the apparent disappearance but then has an impressive "how did he do that" ending when he removes his wallet from his back pocket, and the ring is attached to a loop alongside his keys.

In the lecture, the magician explained how he had been performing this trick for many years and it had become a signature piece of magic that he would perform, especially at weddings and parties where a ring was central to the events of the day. On this one occasion after handing the ring back to the volunteer and receiving rapturous applause for the magic, the volunteer accused him of damaging the ring. There was a placing for four diamonds and one of them was missing. The magician had noticed this when he took the ring, but didn't think anything of it. Now he found himself in the precarious situation where it was being alleged that he had either broken the ring, or at least lost one of the diamonds. This could have been a precious ring, handed down from generation to generation. This magician had public liability insurance and managed to claim on that, but as this forces his annual premiums up it is safe to say that this one performance has cost him thousands of pounds in the following years. Had he not been insured, it's unimaginable what the consequences could have been for his career.

This is why, if I was Stevie Starr, I would certainly switch Amanda's engagement ring for a cheap duplicate during the walk back to the stage. This affords protection from any damage to the ring and means the audience do not get a good look at the actual ring. This is important because if the ring that is swallowed looks nothing like the real ring the audience will know a switch has been made. You can see when Stevie regurgitates the ring on the padlock he keeps it moving by swinging his head, preventing us from having a close look. I suspect that if Stevie can swallow two items and regurgitate either one at will then the padlock with the ring was swallowed beforehand and a duplicate empty padlock is swallowed during the performance to give the illusion that the ring has attached to the padlock inside his body. If Stevie can only swallow and regurgitate one item at a time then it is feasible that the empty padlock is switched with one that already has the dummy ring attached just before he swallows it. However he chooses to carry out the effect, it looks like a brilliant combination of specialist skill and magic secrets to create something like you have never seen before. This is an act you'll remember every time you close your eyes. Truly marvellous, yet disgusting!

Series 5 - 2011

There seemed to be a change in the way magic was shown on Britain's Got Talent from series five. This year a talented magician presented a brand new illusion which brought the house down. A great example of choreography, skill, showmanship and great props gave this series the first example of how exciting magic can be and set the tone of what was to follow. Despite being the only magician in this series, David Penn, a respected and well known magician showed that good magic can get a great audience response and he made it through to the final easily with his professional and accomplished style. From this series on the quantity and quality of the magic performances increased many times over and I imagine that David Penn's performance opened the door to quality magical talent taking the show seriously, along with the judges starting to respect the craft and artistry.

David and Karen - Audition

www.youtube.com/watch?v=IIRRxQsqWAE

In their first audition, David and Karen performed a "blink and you'll miss it" metamorphosis. Up to this point, the most well known of this kind of act was performed by John and Charlotte Pendragon, who had made their trick (called Metamorphosis, funnily enough) the world leader in the instant switch. The main prop in the Pendragon's routine, known as a Sub-Trunk, allowed John to instantly switch places with Charlotte, despite her being in the trunk, tied up in a bag. The instantaneous switch, performed with the speed and dexterity required to create the illusion of an instant change was incredible. Other performers have performed this illusion over the years and no-one I have ever seen comes anywhere near to the quality of the Pendragon's presentation. The comedian Justin Lee-Collins chose to use this trick in his series, "The Convention Crasher" and seeing him struggle to learn the routine in that programme only serves to heighten the appreciation of the Pendragon's incredible performance. In the 1990s, Valentino, the Masked Magician revealed the secret to the sub-trunk, but in his version a curtain needed to be raised three times, when the Pendragons do the whole switch with one, very brief raise of the curtain. The Pendragons performed some of the best magic I have ever seen and it's definitely worth your time to read further about them.

Jump forwards to 2011 and David Penn brought a new, more exciting and impressive version of a similar magical theory. For the audition, David and Karen walked out onto the stage to loud, atmospheric music, and showed the audience one of the biggest pieces of magic apparatus ever seen on the Britain's Got Talent stage. In a change to the traditional gender roles, Karen opened the front of the illusion and David climbed a ladder and squeezed himself into a box. A transparent front cover was slid into place, and David put his hand through a hole in the front. The box was covered with a silver curtain, and David placed his hand through a hole in the curtain so the audience could see that he was still in the box. This was obviously a real hand, and not a robotic replica. As far as anyone could see, David was trapped in the box.

The ladder is removed, and another silver curtain is lifted and shown to be just a regular curtain. David takes hold of one end of a rod at the corner of the curtain and Karen walks away from the box unfolding the curtain and obscuring the left hand side of the illusion. With David's hand still clearly visible, Karen ducks behind the curtain and with the speed of the Pendragons on their best day, Karen has switched placed with David despite him apparently still holding the curtain from within the box! David throws the curtain to the ground and Karen is nowhere to be seen. David whisks the curtain away from the box and we can see that Karen is inside the box, her hand still sticking out through the hole in the front. It's a beautiful illusion.

If you've ever been in a situation where you work hard at something only for someone else to take the credit, you'll feel the pain of David's assistant. Not Karen – she gets all the credit for an excellent performance, but the second assistant. We don't know her name, in fact the only thing we do know about her is what her hand looks like! This is because the illusion is built to house a third member of the team, someone the audience never sees. Earlier in the explanations we looked at the fake tabletop which appears thinner that it really is by masking the size with black and silver trim. A similar visual illusion is in use here, with box seemingly resting at the top of a thin silver post. The reality is that the bottom of the box is considerably wider that you may realise, and the post has a thick black shadow on both sides of the silver decoration – certainly wide enough to hold the secret third person.

When David climbs into the box, he places his hand through the hole, and when the curtain covers the box his hand appears through that as well so we can see he is still in the box. In reality as the curtain drapes over the front of the box David removes his hand from the hole and the mystery third person stick her hand out of the top of the silver pillar and through the curtain. The audience assume this is David's hand but as he is completely obscured from view he is now free to climb down from the box and hide behind Karen's curtain. In the video above, David has about five seconds to get from the box to behind the curtain, and I suspect that the use of booming music serves to disguise any noise that may result as he climbs down. As Karen ducks down, David jumps up and the switch appears complete. There is another five seconds or so when Karen is out of sight to get her back into the box, and as David removes the curtain the third team member removes their hand from the hole in the curtain and Karen places hers through the hole in the box. This trick I feel would be fairly obvious if performed by less talented magicians but the split second timing and apparent hours of rehearsal make this a delight to watch.

David and Karen – Semi Final

www.youtube.com/watch?v=s6ANQv4WJfk

For the Semi Final, David and Karen performed a similar routine but with another extremely impressive prop box and great choreography and timing. Similar to their audition but with an element of apparent danger, Karen is handcuffed and shut inside another specially designed piece of magical apparatus, this time a glass box filled with water. It appears that Karen is in the water a long time, but the reality is that the locked box can be freely opened behind the curtain, with Karen able to leap out when she needs to. Meanwhile, David can slide in from above and the excellent timing presents the illusion that everything happened in an instant. Karen could of course exit the box at any time when the curtain was lowered. Whilst this trick takes more technical skill than the audition, the overall effect I felt was a little weaker and sadly, David and Karen did not make it to the final. The judges' comments were excellent, and this did seem to herald the point where Britain's Got Talent started to take magic seriously.

Series 6 - 2012

Continuing the movement towards presenting quality magic done well, Brynolf and Ljung, two highly respected performers made their BGT debut in 2012. Sailing through the auditions, they demonstrated once again that magic is an art form and can be so much more than the stuff you see at children's parties and on cruise ships. Simon's initial reaction to the first audition was the last time in the series that we see him hating a card trick before he's even seen it, and like David Penn earlier, Brynolf and Ljung continued to show the viewing audience that magic can be hugely entertaining when done well.

Brynolf and Ljung - Audition

www.youtube.com/watch?v=hSd1wLStkKE

Peter Brynolf takes a lot of punishment during this performance but it's worth it. As a demonstration of a simple magical principle raised to world class performance through quality presentation this is one of the best examples on Britain's Got Talent. Ljung takes a roll of thick grey Duct Tape and wraps it around Brynolf's head, obscuring his eyes and mouth. The tape appears tight, and it will surely be painful to remove later! Ljung then heads to the judges with a pack of playing cards, and asks David Walliams to remove and sign one card. He asks Amanda Holden to name a number between one and fifteen. With a random card chosen and a random number given, it's up to Brynolf to shuffle the pack and make that card appear at that location in the deck. Brynolf theatrically flings cards around on stage counting to twelve, the chosen number. When the card at that location is revealed it is the wrong card. This creates the perfect off-beat moment, especially as two of the judges, assuming the trick has gone wrong, buzz their buzzers to show their dissatisfaction. However the trick has not failed, as Brynolf takes a small pair of scissors and cuts away the Duct Tape, revealing the card is in his mouth – the same card, signed by David Walliams earlier.

This trick combines the magician's secret of the Mercury Fold with excellent use of off-beat timing and distraction. The Mercury Fold involves shuffling a pack of cards and using card control skills to move the selected card to the bottom of the deck. Once there, it can be folded into four with the deck obscuring the movement from the audience. My favourite shuffle method is to cut the deck into two piles, place the chosen card on top of the bottom pile, then put the top half of the pack back on top whilst holding the little finger in the space between the two halves. The pack looks solid, but the magician is holding that break using their finger. Magicians call this the pinkie-break. Then the cards can be cut, bringing the chosen card to the top of the pack, then shuffled with the top card being dragged to be the first that falls in the overhand shuffle. Once the card is at the bottom of the deck, the pack can be held in the hand quite naturally, covering the movement of the fingertips that drag the shorter edge of the bottom card towards the back of the deck, folding the card in two. Once this is done the fingertips drag the longer edge so the card is folded into four. This Mercury Fold is carried out in full view of the audience with the deck of cards obscuring the folding taking place underneath. When the cards are handed to Brynolf, he performs the fold in the off-beat when the trick has appeared to go wrong. The folded card is hidden in the left hand and the deck is in the right hand.

This is where the abuse comes in. Ljung says that Brynolf was "not even close!" and suddenly slaps him on the back of the head, causing his head to fall forward. He leans completely forward, dropping all the cards from the right hand whilst putting the folded card in his mouth. However, you may be thinking that this is not possible because his mouth is covered with tape. The TV broadcast did come with a "do not try this at home" disclaimer and I would not recommend it. However, there are some brands of tape that are not as sticky as you may expect and with the movement of the skin, sweat and grease makes the tape much more fluid than you may imagine it would be. This is useful for the magician because the smallest movements of the mouth are obscured by the tape, so it is difficult to see that the tape is covering the mouth but isn't stuck to it. The thickness of the tape prevents it snagging or sticking to itself when the mouth comes loose. Other methods include using a pre-prepared piece of tape with paper stuck to the part that would normally be in contact with the mouth, or simply wearing a big smile when the tape is applied which means the tape is taught against the skin until the smile becomes a frown that loosens the tape enough for the trick to work. The card is popped into the mouth and the magic is complete.

Brynolf and Ljung – Semi Final

www.youtube.com/watch?v=Jjv3yNKxdgM

For the semi final, Brynolf and Ljung did one of my favourite performances of the whole eleven years of Britain's Got Talent. For this, Alicia Dixon was asked to choose a DVD from a transparent bag that clearly contained a variety of DVD movies. The audience can see recognisable logos such as Ghostbusters and other well known movies, and Alicia reached into the bag and removed a Harry Potter DVD.

This set the theme for what was to follow, with a miraculous apparition of a lady cellist, followed by a whole band of violin players, then a prediction that the movie choice would indeed be Harry Potter, followed by an astonishing metamorphosis as Peter instantly changed from one place to another, with the person we thought was Peter becoming Harry Potter!

To understand the complexity of this trick you need to know about a very simple prop. The magician's Force Bag as it is known, is a very convincing illusion. At the start of the routine the force bag can be seen to contain many DVDs and I would guess that these movies were picked to be instantly recognisable from a distance. To the untrained eye, any DVD could have been chosen and this would have required the band to know music from each film and to have a lookalike character for every possible outcome. To make life easier the force bag is manufactured in three distinct sections. The left and right section make up the visible walls of the bag, and these are sealed closed with the DVDs inside. From the outside the bag looks full but upon reaching inside the bag would be empty. The middle section is then filled with multiple Harry Potter DVDs and the effect is complete. Alicia is presented with a big bag filled with a mixture of DVDs but the only ones that can be felt inside and removed are the Harry Potter movies.

When the magicians move up to the stage, the next part of the trick is another lesson in expert choreography. The chair is a specific magician's prop that can hide the assistant inside. When the curtain is raised the assistant can quickly move from the hidden position inside the chair to be sat down in very little time. What impressed me about this section was that as an audience member I had seen this trick many times and expected the reveal of the cello player to be the only person revealed. Brilliantly, Brynolf and Ljung take this one step further by revealing the first musician with a grand swish of the curtain, which they make fall across the back of the stage, obscuring the next location where the following musicians will appear from. The movement is so precise, yet so casual that it does not seem that the curtain is set up for another reveal and this is why the other band members catch you by surprise. All that's really happening is the band members are behind the raised stage and step up behind the curtain but it's so well done and doesn't seem forced – a magnificent piece of magic.

Following this, the magicians reveal the prediction that the movie choice would be Harry Potter by revealing two large rectangular displays that display a question mark when pushed together. The question mark is printed on a sheet which is removed to reveal the image of Harry Potter's glasses. This is where the final piece of magical choreography takes place. Brynolf and Ljung reveal their prediction, with Ljung on the left and Peter on the right. Secretly there is a Harry Potter lookalike dressed as Peter behind one of the rectangular displays. Ljung keeps hold of his half of the question mark curtain sheet and rotates it to a landscape orientation with the right hand end lined up with the display. Peter moves behind the display and sneaks unknown behind Ljung's sheet. Meanwhile the Harry Potter lookalike is dressed in the same suit as Peter so the audience believe that Peter is merely moving to the left in order to slide the display off stage to the right. He pushes the display away then runs to the centre of the stage. With the audience still believing this is Peter, Ljung whisks away the curtain to reveal Peter is with him, and as the audience attention moves towards both magicians, the imposter on stage turns around to reveal he is wearing the full Harry Potter costume on the front of his body with the suit either ditched or just covering his back. Either way it's a fantastic piece of misdirection and a brilliant finale. Sadly despite the amazing audience reaction and brilliant judges' comments, Brynolf and Ljung did not get through to the final and this was their last Britain's Got Talent performance. However this was not the end of their TV talent show journey as they have appeared in other "Got Talent" shows around the world since, always receiving a great reaction from the audience and judges.

Series 7 – 2013

James More – Audition

www.youtube.com/watch?v=pVmp1cc2Wxo

James More is another well respected magical artiste, and for series seven James pulled out another large scale illusion. With the dance moves and good looks, James set the standard for exciting and enjoyable performance. Along with David Penn in series five, James demonstrated the kind of magical performance I was used to seeing in the high-end live shows and was as far removed from the balloon modelling, spoon bending, kids birthday party image that magic is known for. Suddenly magic was becoming cool.

For this trick, James was lifted onto what appeared to be a sword and was somehow balanced on top of the sharp tip as he slowly spun around. The audience is left thinking, "how is he not getting impaled on that spike?" when suddenly, yes, you've guessed it, he gets impaled on that spike! The effect is phenomenal – the audience is taken by surprise and as James is lifted off the spike (during a very distant camera angle for the TV broadcast) the audience response is incredible. He's unharmed, the "accident" was part of the illusion and James sailed through to the semi final rounds.

This illusion, also made famous by David Copperfield and the Pendragons, is known as "Impaled" and is most commonly attributed to the inventor Ken Whitaker in the 1970s. The most widely recognised method for this illusion involves the performer wearing a harness or corset which is hidden by his clothes. The Pendragon's version of this effect is often considered the most impressive as Charlotte Pendragon wears such skimpy costumes it would seem impossible for her to conceal such a corset. As the assistant is lifted onto the sword, the tip engages into a mechanism which links the sword to the corset. The back of the corset is usually made of metal so the effect is that the corset and sword combine to become a solid table which the magician is laying on. As the magician slowly rotates on this platform, the moment arrives when the performer is to be impaled on the sword. At this point, another mechanism is operated which causes the sword to drop down into the base of the apparatus, and at exactly the same moment a duplicate sword tip shoots out of the top of the corset. As we have seen in previous explanations music is often used to disguise the sound of the mechanism, or to provide cues to an off-stage partner who controls the activation of the illusion.

With the invention of the internet and international online shopping there has been an increase in the number of dealers around the world that manufacture fake or copied versions of magician's props and it may surprise you to see how cheaply an illusion that looks like this can be obtained. Be aware with this trick that the force of the drop could cause injury if the equipment is not perfectly designed, and well-engineered props are important with this illusion to avoid potentially serious injury. The magician lays on such a small platform to give the impression that they are bent over backwards on the spike that there can be a risk of injury that is increased if the workmanship of the prop is cheap and substandard. As an aspiring magician it can be very tempting to look online and purchase imitation props from suppliers as far away as China, and recently a movement of magicians began a campaign known as "don't copy the magic", with dealers at conventions proudly displaying signs to confirm that everything they sell is the original product and not a cheap copy.

Copyright law is often ignored by the companies that churn out imitations and this can be devastating for the one-man-band performers that make their own illusions. A very good example of this is the story of Dirk Losander, a man who invented the Anti-Gravity Floating Table. Having met Losander a number of times, I can confirm that the workmanship and quality of his range of tables is streets ahead of any others I have seen, and they are well worth the investment. A quick internet search reveals websites selling their own copy versions of his floating table, some using his own photographs from his website, and one even showing a video of the table in action, being demonstrated by Losander himself! You can rest assured that these tables, sometimes as cheap as one fifth of the price of the real thing, are not the same product at all. They do not float in the same way and the overall effect is weak. Sadly, the proliferation of the cheap knock-offs on the market means that the table trick is widely used, and many people think they have seen the trick performed in cabaret. It's only when you see Losander performing the routine personally that you see the real magic.

James More on the other hand is obviously using the genuine equipment, and this magnificent performance saw him straight through to the semi finals.

James More – Semi Final

www.youtube.com/watch?v=XqvucHS42nY

For the semi final, we return to more familiar territory, with an effect achieved with similar methods to previous routines we have examined.

James appears on stage with a flaming torch in hand and another massive stage illusion. We see spikes, fire, danger, excitement and this illusion ticks a lot of the boxes. However, we also see our old favourite, the thin table with a silver strip that disguises the thickness of the surface. Upon examining the platform that James lays down on, we can see that rather than being the thin metal table that it appears to be, there is actually a V shaped area underneath which looks big enough to contain a person.

In a great twist on the traditional magic performance, James does a teleportation to a different area of the studio, similar to Sauris Nandi's illusion that was performed with twins. I would expect that James' illusion when performed as per the manufacturer's instructions involves the magician dropping into the hidden V shaped compartment before the spikes drop down. The audience would believe that he has been speared by the fiery spikes then the curtain would be removed to show he has magically disappeared instead. James looks to have improved on this illusion by adding the teleportation. We apparently see James performing his escape from the shackles as we can see his shadow cast onto the curtain. As soon as the spikes drop we can see he has vanished and within seconds he is stood behind the judges blowing an air-horn to attract the audience's attention. So how did he get there so quickly?

The answer seems to lie in yet another un-credited magician's assistant. Just as David Penn had a second hidden assistant that we are not supposed to know about, James has an assistant hidden in the V shaped area of the apparatus. As soon as the curtain drops, James can escape out of the back of the equipment under the cover of the clever lighting. The extra performer comes out of the hidden area and mimes the escape from the shackles. In shadow there is no perception of depth and this allows the assistant to mime the escape either in front or behind where the spikes will fall. The illusion will appear as if the spikes went straight through the assistant, but they could be arranged to fall around him. As the spikes fall, the assistant can drop down back into the hidden area. This whole process has provided the much needed time for James to get into position. With all attention on the stage, James simply waits in position and draw attention to himself with the air-horn at the right moment.

In the Paul Daniels book, More Magic, Paul mentions a cheeky little song he would sing to himself when performing card tricks, "hey diddle diddle, we're working a fiddle". In big stage illusion, as soon as the curtain is raised you can be sure that something funny is going on.

Stevie Pink - Audition

www.youtube.com/watch?v=3CEUUyFcKBY

As camp as Christmas and dressed from head to toe in shocking pink, Stevie Pink caught the judges attention although it was touch and go for a second. Stevie danced with his beautiful assistant before clicking his fingers to put her in a trance. Two of the judges took an instant dislike at this point with a loud press of the buzzers. It's true that this approach ("I can put you in a trance with just a click of the fingers! I am amazing") is extremely cheesy and straight out of the cruise-ship magician's handbook. However Stevie goes on to perform a fairly impressive levitation routine with a number of clever tricks to throw the audience off the scent of how it's done. Although this is an off-the-shelf illusion that doesn't take a great deal of skill to perform, the additional use of the hula hoop to demonstrate there is apparently nothing holding the assistant in the air really works to sell this illusion.

Britain's Got Talent producers are very good at directing the TV broadcast to mimic the audience's own misdirection with cutaways to audience and judges reactions that mask the moments where the audience at home might see the secret. In this performance we see the assistant is laid onto the table, but we do not see Stevie Pink stepping behind her. If we did, we may see that the table surface is not part of the platform you can see from the front but is a separate table entirely. The support for this table is behind where Stevie stands and his body hides this from view. The platform that the assistant lays on is connected to the support behind Stevie on his left side near his belt. As the two halves of the table are folded down, the mechanism lifts the assistant higher with the platform in front of the magician, the lifting mechanism behind him, and the link between the performer's chest and underarm. You can see the way the show has been edited, cutting to the judges reaction as the assistant rotates around the body of the magician. The link piece from front to back is obscured by the magician's outstretched arms, and this is slightly visible on closer inspection. It appears that the mechanism may have been more clearly noticeable at points, requiring a brief cutaway to a judge to mask it from the audience.

But if there's a strong, thick, supporting piece of metal running from the platform to behind Stevie, how does he pass the hoop over the assistant's entire body? The simple secret here is that he passes the hoop around the assistant, not across the assistant, which is a subtle difference which creates an optical illusion. The hoop is passed to Stevie who has to remain standing on the spot to disguise the mechanism, and he holds up the hoop level with the assistant's feet. He then passes the hoop from one end of the assistant across to the other, with the side of the hoop that is nearest the audience passing the full length of her body. Meanwhile the side of the hoop nearest the magician makes almost the same journey but stops when it would hit the barrier of the metal bar. The front of the hoop passes over the assistant's head, and the hoop is passed behind the assistant back to the feet, apparently to make a second sweep across. In fact now the front of the hoop is on the other side of the barrier, and the back of the hoop can now be rotated over the feet. It looks like the hoop has passed over the assistant twice, but in reality the hoop is being rotated around the barrier and the back of the hoop (nearest the magician) never makes a complete pass across the assistant due to the barrier.

Stevie Pink – Semi Final

www.youtube.com/watch?v=nu5su7RnzCc

Stevie upped the camp quotient for the semi final, making a man on a motorbike appear as if from nowhere. To me, Stevie squandered any chance he had of making it to the finals with such a simple trick. With terrible camp comedy, jokes about being in the closet, and the apparition of a topless man on the motorbike, this was one of the worst magical performances I have ever seen and I have no idea why he chose this routine for the semi final. It seems to me that the cabinet curtains have plenty of space behind them even when apparently fully opened, lots of room to conceal the pieces of the motorbike and the man or men that fit them all together. I hope this illusion didn't cost a lot of money as for me it didn't impress at all, and didn't make it to the final.

Series 8 – 2014

As Britain's Got Talent continued to grow to love magic as a legitimate form of entertainment, Series eight brought us the fabulous Darcy Oake. Already well respected by magicians, Darcy travelled from Canada to be on the show. Simon described him as "without question, the best magician ever on Britain's Got Talent" and with two successful performances on the show Darcy became the first magician to make it to the final. Whilst he did not win overall his performances were hugely popular with his first audition being viewed 67 million times on YouTube. Truly, magic had now come of age in the show, in the following series there were multiple magicians all following on from Darcy's success.

Darcy Oake – Audition

www.youtube.com/watch?v=gO_KyTtJg10

Darcy chose an absolute classic of magic for his first Britain's Got Talent performance. Dove production dates back centuries, but the Las Vegas magician, Lance Burton, made it his signature routine. Lance performed at the Monte Carlo hotel on the Vegas strip for fifteen years with one of the most accomplished acts I have ever seen. Lance is known as the magician's magician, and for anyone wanting to see a master at work his show was not to be missed. I saw the show on three occasions during the 1990s and I don't think I have ever seen a more perfect demonstration of magic as an art form. I have seen many magicians performing with doves over the years and none have captured the beauty of Lance's act. His control of the birds as they flew over the audience was incredible, and the way he made the birds both appear and disappear at will was superb.

The skill required to perform the dove production needs to take into account the dove's welfare as well as the audience reaction. During an audition show for the FISM World Championships of Magic I saw an act booed off stage by the audience that was predominantly made up of magicians. This can be the toughest audience, and whilst the performance seemed good, the audience disagreed. Many of the magicians in the crowd know the secrets and the speed with which this performer was working suggested that the birds were being mistreated. The curtain came down over the stage and the magician was not seen again in the competition.

In Darcy's audition the audience can see there is a cage on a table on stage. This is not just an ordinary birdcage but a specific magician's prop that can be purchased from magic dealers. This will be used later in the trick and is more than just a place for the birds to be put during the performance.

The first illusion involves the magician's favourite prop, flash string. As mentioned previously flash string is coated in special chemicals that make it burn to ash whilst producing a huge flash. Paper, wool and other products can be purchased from magic dealers, all producing the same illusion when set alight – a huge flash and no trace of the wool, paper or string afterwards. As with the Deans of Magic, who made a necklace appear, Darcy uses the distraction of the flash to produce the first dove, which is hidden in a tube up his left sleeve.

It is worth discussion at this point as to why doves have been used for so many years by magicians. The unusual thing about doves is that they are a sort of natural optical illusion! They are fairly large birds with a wide wingspan and when they fly from the stage the audience are amazed and wonder where on earth did these huge birds come from? If you see a dove close up in a cage it is surprising to see that the body of the dove is actually very small, and the key to the magician's performance is this discrepancy in the perception of the size of a dove by an audience. Doves can fold their head under their wing happily and comfortably. Also, doves are naturally very docile creatures. It may sound cruel to put a dove in a toilet roll tube for example, but it would fit comfortably, would not struggle to get out and would not be distressed by the ordeal. Also, upon removal from the tube, the natural instinct of the bird is to spread their wings, which is great for the magical effect of a large bird apparently appearing from nowhere.

The illusions come thick and fast in this routine, with another dove being pulled from the other sleeve, under the cover of the first dove. This effect is stunning as it appears that the dove has somehow been pulled apart to make two birds, but the reality is that the second bird was produced in much the same way as the first.

The show direction follows the misdirection intended by the magician and there are a number of audience and judge reaction shots inserted to mask the moments that would be hard to see in a live situation but easier to spot on television. When we see Darcy again his hand is in place to reveal the next dove which is loaded inside the jacket, whilst he misdirects the audience with a white silk handkerchief in the other hand. The audience's attention is drawn to the bright coloured silk which is attached by elastic to the inside of the jacket. The silk shoots behind and the bird comes out and the illusion is that the silk turned into the dove. The hand really is quicker than the eye.

As this dove is placed into the cage, something is loaded into Darcy's other hand from under the sleeve of the jacket. This looks like it's the egg that will appear after the next bird production.

Another bird appears from the sleeve using the same technique as before, and the egg is dropped from the other hand to make the illusion that the bird just laid the egg!

Another bird is produced from the sleeve and then a magic prop birdcage is produced in the same way. This specially designed item is spring loaded and folds small and flat and can be incorporated into the dove production tricks using the same secrets as the birds. You can see from the audience reaction that they cannot believe that there is enough room for all these birds to be secreted around one person, but everything folds small – the cage, the birds, and the second birdcage which is produced in the same way as the earlier effect where a dove appeared to be split into two.

For the final illusion, the trick birdcage table is used. Darcy stands behind the table and we can see another optical illusion is taking place. We assume the birdcage to be transparent all the way around and the reason we cannot see through is because of the black curtain that has been draped over the top of the cage. In fact, the cage is only about half as deep as it might appear and the back wall of the cage is made from the same material as the table surface. Also on the table but hiding behind the cage is the magician's assistant. To give the illusion that the depth of the cage was roughly the depth of the table, a frame is sewn into the curtain of the dimensions that the audience expects to see. Darcy covers the table with the curtain and as soon as the cage is obscured from view the assistant plays her part. Darcy lifts the frame that is part of the curtain, and the assistant pushes the back wall of the cage which rotates into the table, the back wall now forming the table surface with the birds safely inside the table. The frame in the curtain makes it appear that the cage is still in place, being lifted up by Darcy. The curtain is the shaken with a theatrical wave and the assistant stands up to rapturous applause from the audience.

As I mentioned earlier I have seen many dove acts and enjoyed this one especially, as it was accomplished beautifully without causing me any reason for concern about the welfare of the animals. The high standards of performance guaranteed Darcy a place in the semi finals.

Darcy Oake – Semi Final

www.youtube.com/watch?v=mmLLkpL6VU4

Regular viewers of Britain's Got Talent, especially those with good memories may have been surprised to see the stage set up for Darcy's semi final routine. Only two years earlier, Brynolf and Ljung performed this very same trick as one part of a much larger routine, in which they magically conjured up an orchestra to play the music of Harry Potter. However, Darcy's take is a magnificent demonstration of magical thinking as the presentation of this effect is almost entirely different to the previous version and has a killer ending that gets a great reaction from the crowd. As you will recall from the Brynolf and Ljung explanation the chair on stage is a special prop chair which is designed to be able to conceal an assistant. The traditional performance allows the magician to cover the empty chair with a curtain and whisk the curtain away to reveal the assistant that apparently magically appeared from nowhere. In Darcy's version, the chair is shown empty as before but this time Darcy himself sits in the chair. I thought, like I assume any other magicians watching would, that Darcy would transform into a beautiful assistant in the chair swapping places with the assistant, but it was not to be. Darcy disappeared all right, and the chair was shown to be empty. In a fantastic piece of showmanship one of the camera crew removed their hat and revealed that they were Darcy Oake – and the audience went crazy. No-one saw that coming and it was an excellent surprise ending.

The magical thinking on display in this routine takes a simple trick that fans of the show saw two years ago and makes it into something considerably bigger. Darcy explains at the beginning of the routine that the TV camera will not cut away and everything you see on your television really is exactly as it is happening on stage. This set up is perfect because it justifies there being a camera man on stage, and we stop paying attention to him. We suspect the dancers, the assistants, but the cameraman is nothing important, when the reality is that the cameraman becomes the point of the entire trick.

With Darcy in the chair and the curtain covering him, a similar technique that was used by the Deans of Magic comes into play to create the effect that Darcy is still sat in the chair. A shell sewn into the curtain looks like the top of the performers head, and shapes are pushed into the curtain from the inside to look like Darcy is still seated. He moves into the secret area in the chair, and the cameraman starts to walk behind the chair giving the illusion that he is filming so Darcy cannot slip out of the back side of the stage. Of course what is happening is that Darcy is hiding his jacket, donning the cameraman's cap, and it is the cameraman who hides in the secret compartment of the chair. All that remains is for Darcy to walk from behind the chair continuing in the same direction and speed as the cameraman was walking, holding the camera, as if he is the same person. As the curtain is removed the audience gasp at the empty chair, and assume that this reveal is the highlight to a pretty standard trick. But Darcy is one step ahead of everyone as he reveals that he is the cameraman. The switch feels like it was instantaneous, because we still saw what we believed to be the magician under the curtain in the chair, right up until the last moment. We feel like we saw the cameraman transform into Darcy before our very eyes! What we didn't see was the switch took place much earlier, in the darkness behind the stage and the chair.

Darcy Oake - Final

https://www.youtube.com/watch?v=kOMtTE9rE1s

It's only my personal opinion of course, but having seen hundreds of magic performances over the years I cannot understand why Darcy would perform an escapology act like this one for the final. This is the act that you future success hinges on. An audience of millions are tuning in and you do… this?

During the 2012 FISM World Championships of Magic I spent four full days sat in the Blackpool Opera House watching over 150 magicians performing their acts. I saw lots of doves, lots of ladies being stuffed into boxes on tables and many many card tricks. The best of these performers brought showmanship and personality to the proceedings but the competition had more than its fair share of people who'd browsed through the magic catalogue, spent a lot of money on a large scale illusion and performed it as per the supplied instructions. After seeing so many acts I started to switch off completely when the stage curtains opened to reveal some elaborate torture device with moody lighting and thumping music.

To give an example of how it should be done, there is a magician called Prince of Illusions, who takes the large scale props and adds a huge amount of magical thinking. His act is one of my all time favourites because he has taken these props and worked out how to fit them into an exciting story with an enjoyable narrative. In his most well known routine he enters the stage dressed in pyjamas, sets an alarm clock and goes to bed. Suddenly the blankets are thrown up into the air and the magician is instantly transformed into a female vampire! The show continues as Michael travels through a nightmare, is trapped and tortured by the vampires and in the end, wakes up in his bed as if waking from his bad dream. The show is stunning, and the inventiveness of the thinking changes the focus of the show entirely. No-one says "I am now going to ask my beautiful assistant to climb into this box", and there are no top hats worn, no tails, no sparkly costumes. The performance is more theatre than magic, even though the props used are magical props.

The Human Bear-Trap used by Darcy Oake in the Britain's Got Talent final seemed to be the exact opposite of the inventiveness of Prince of Illusions. The audience is meant to be impressed by the massive apparatus hanging from the ceiling, and maybe they are. Perhaps I am jaded having seen so much magic in my life. But my expectation would be that as Darcy announces that we are about to see him climb into a Human Bear-Trap, the audience think, "What the hell is a Human Bear-Trap?"

Seriously – have you ever seen one of these before? Where could you buy one? What is it for? Is there a need in the hunting community to make a trap suitable for humans and bears alike? Of course there isn't which is what makes me leap to the conclusion that what we are seeing is specially made magical apparatus. And, if this device is made entirely for this purpose, you can bet your life that it's got all the safety mechanisms in place to avoid the loss of life so heavily expressed as possible by the performer.

If the magician is at no real risk of injury from the ridiculous oversized Human Bear-Trap then what is the point of the whole spectacle – drama? Exactly how much drama can there be if there's no danger?

As with every other act of this type that I have seen, the trap is set on fire (as if being pierced all over your body by spikes is somehow more deadly if the spikes are on fire) and Darcy, wrapped tightly in a strait-jacket just like Merlin Cadogan all those years ago on Britain's Got Talent, is raised to hang upside down between the (so we're told) deadly spikes that could kill this poor innocent magician.

Again, we see how the director of the programme uses misdirection to obscure the crucial moment that could giveaway the method used for the escape. We can see that Darcy's hands are tied behind his back in the strait-jacket, and despite lots of wriggling around nothing much seems to happen for the first thirty seconds or so. Then, at exactly the right moment, the camera changes to a shot of the crane and when we see Darcy again just a second or two later, his arms are completely loose. My suggestion is that this is a gimmicked strait-jacket which the performer can pull loose at any time. Darcy can then remove the straight-jacket completely and unhook his feet. Without the Human Bear-Trap this act would be much the same as Merlin Cadogan performed in series 3 but in this example I feel that less is more. By keeping the apparatus simple, Merlin escaped from the strait-jacket before the burning rope broke and this escape looked like real skill. In Darcy's version the ridiculous apparatus (to me at least) detracts from the skill on display, because – don't get me wrong – this is still a very difficult act to perform. It requires enormous upper body strength, the performer is still hanging upside down, and the pressure to do this whilst watching the timer and getting out of the shackles with seconds to spare requires a very talented magician to carry this off. But for me, it feels like a by-the-numbers cabaret routine. We all know he's not going to die, there's probably a release mechanism that is pressed to make the jaws of the trap slam shut when we can see he is clear away, and even if he couldn't get out and ended up trapped would the TV regulators Ofcom allow this to go out before watershed on live television? Maybe I'm jaded – the audience seemed to love it. He didn't win though. Perhaps he should have done a card trick, as we'll see in series nine.

Series 9 – 2015

After eight years, the series had seen only one magician reach the final, and still no magic act had ever won Britain's Got Talent. Series nine changed that as we finally got a runner up in the form of Jamie Raven, again a respected magician, but this time a contestant known for close-up magic. This is a departure for the show as all the magic seen so far had been big stage illusions. Magicians rely on showmanship and performance to sell that illusion as magic to the audience. In close-up the magicians use dexterity and years of practice to make miracles happen and in the age of TV Hard Drive Recorders it's easy to go back and frame by frame look for any tiny imperfection in the act. Close-up is my favourite type of magic and it was great to see Jamie Raven do so well. Even the simplest of tricks were performed to such a great reaction and it really showed me that with showmanship and presentation a trick deck of cards that you can pick up on eBay can get you a long way on a TV talent show.

Chloe Louise Crawford – Audition

www.youtube.com/watch?v=pFvrRY60lw0

Chloe Louise Crawford, a magicians assistant in Las Vegas but originally from Portsmouth joined Britain's Got Talent in the hope of stepping out from the magicians shadow to take the lead herself. This is not the leap you might imagine as often the assistant performs the most difficult part of the big stage illusion, cramming themselves into tight spaces and working hard facilitating the secret to the trick whilst out of sight of the audience.

For the audition, Chloe appears to have borrowed Stevie Pink's motorbike which, for reasons that are not made clear is in a large wooden crate. There's no reason for this, and therefore we can assume that the crate has a role in the method. Chloe dons a crash helmet which seems odd because she's not really going very far, and gets onto the motorbike. She drives over to another piece of magical apparatus and this is lifted high into the air. A distracting explosion and the bottom falls out of the platform she was on and the bike and rider seem to have vanished. Instantly, Chloe and the bike have vanished from the stage and reappeared in the Royal Box. How did they get there so quickly?

This routine is a classic of magic, famously performed in the 1970s and 1980s by the hugely successful magician Doug Henning. The Britain's Got Talent method appears identical to the TV broadcast from 1981, where Doug performs the trick alongside funky dancers, bright rainbow coloured sets and bouncy music. It's the single most 1980s thing you have ever seen and is on YouTube if you'd like to check it out.

In Doug's version, there is a rainbow running across the stage that forms part of a motorcycle track. In the middle of the rainbow there is a box which is of similar dimensions to Chloe's crate. To the left there is the same apparatus for both magicians, which will lift them high into the air before vanishing them completely.

Most people did not have video recorders in 1981. Back then, you'd see the trick and be amazed, but if you did have the ability to go back and watch a second time you would work it out immediately. In the original trick, Doug introduces himself to the audience, then dons a crash helmet and assists the dancers in demonstrating the box in the centre of the rainbow. The box is assembled and as soon as the front of the box is raised, Doug ducks behind just for a second. We know that this has to be a switch and the crash helmet does a great job at concealing that the man we are all focussing on is not Doug Henning any more. A hidden duplicate bike is lifted into the box from behind which Doug sits on ready to drive out later. Meanwhile our Doug-a-like has ridden the original bike into the other box which is now being lifted into the air.

At the point of the explosion, the floor of the box drops open, but this is not the real floor. It seems that what you see swinging below the hanging box is a duplicate floor on a hinge which drops down. At the same time, a black curtain falls from the front of the box. This covers the spaces through the pattern on the front of the box and hides the lookalike and motorbike from view. The lighting is very dim and this also helps the illusion. As we can see the floor has apparently given way and can no longer see the magician, we assume they have disappeared but before we have a chance to think the other box is opened which contains the real Doug Henning and the duplicate bike.

For Chloe on Britain's Got Talent, an act like this would be pulled apart by furious Twitter uses that expect and demand real magic! They would watch the footage a second time and say, "It's easy! She put on the crash helmet, and went behind the box for no reason at all, then came out and it was a lookalike!" (Although they would have to abbreviate that into 140 characters somehow). Back in 1981 you only had one chance to see the switch but now this routine wouldn't cut it on TV. The live performance would be fine and the audience would love it, but to make it work for a TV audience there needs to be some clever editing. Sure enough, on repeated viewings you can see that something is not quite right. It would appear that Chloe dons the crash helmet and starts to step behind the crate as the camera cuts to the judges looking on. When the camera comes back to Chloe she is already in position ready to get on the bike. That's definitely not Chloe, but unless she's using a twin (like Sauris Nandi) it makes sense that the TV broadcast cut away when the switch took place.

Chloe now has all the time she needs to get into the Royal Box where a duplicate motorbike has been waiting all along. After all, with the lights not shining on the Royal Box, no-one's going to have looked up there or been able to see anything, until the lights go up and Chloe is sat on the bike.

Chloe Louise Crawford – Semi Final

www.youtube.com/watch?v=LczWcvDcX5g

The judges' comments for this act were harsh, but I agree with them – I was expecting more. Beautifully choreographed and brilliantly performed it was only at the end of the act that I realised there wasn't a lot to see. As Chloe levitated her male assistant I was impressed at how high in the air he had gone, and when Chloe followed him up there I have to say, I didn't see that coming. But for all of that, I much preferred Stevie Pink's levitation and chuckled a little at the two acts being worlds apart, yet both doing motorbike tricks for the audition and levitation for the semi's – perhaps they are brother and sister? I have to say that if this trick was performed in the street it would have blown me away, but to see two people lifted up and put down again on a dark stage, in a dark theatre against a black background really didn't do it for me. After seeing David Copperfield performing his famous flying routine at the MGM theatre in Las Vegas, this looked a really simple trick by comparison. As both acts use wires and harnesses to make their performers float, the beauty and artistry on display when Copperfield performs really take your breath away. I showed this clip to my eight year old niece who was blown away by the performance. I then showed her Chloe's act and she turned to me and said, "Is she on a string?" The audience didn't send Chloe through to the final, although I would have been interested to see what she would have come up with, given the opportunity.

Michael Late – Audition

www.youtube.com/watch?v=_AK0yxd04js

Here's another great example of where less is more. In the tightly edited audition, Michael races through three tricks in such a short space of time that the audience barely has the opportunity to focus on how incredible it all is. Compare for example the first few seconds of this audition with a group of French performers known as Cubic Act. Michael's audition starts with a Cooper's barrel standing on a platform which rocks on its own, levitates in front of one of the assistants, before Michael mysteriously appears with his head sticking out of the top of the barrel – while it's still floating! This is a cool trick, but then Michael gets out of the barrel and moves on to the next effect. Cubic Act on the other hand get their entire routine from the same magical principle, by presenting a clever piece of performance art which uses a floating box instead of a barrel. The trick is the same, but Cubic Act take it slow. From a magical perspective you only see the one trick, but it's beautiful. Puzzling, exciting, quirky and performed brilliantly, Cubic Act's version of this trick stays with you for a long time and is one of the best pieces of performance art I have seen. Most people watching Cubic Act would not consider that they just saw a magician, because their style is so unique.

The method for this trick is one that is quite unbelievable when you learn it, because the effect is too good to believe that it is so simple. Thinking back to Stevie Pink's levitation, the assistant lay on a platform that was attached to the base by a strong metal stand, obscured by the performer who stood between the platform and the stand. The same is true of this trick, with the performer sat on a small platform attached to the base. The assistant takes their place between the stand and the box, obscuring it from view when the box is levitated. Lighting and scenery also disguise the stand which is only visible when the box is lifted anyway. There is room in top half of the box / barrel for the hidden performer inside to hide when the box is resting on the platform. The magician inside can lift the box, rotate it and put it back without revealing himself, then stick his head out of the top when he wants to. As with so many tricks discussed here, this is another perfect example of how the performance of the trick makes it such an amazing illusion, even though the secret is simple.

Another great example of the optical illusion built into the design of great magical props is the Accordion Squisher. The magician is placed into the box and his head is forced through a hole at the top. The box is then rolled upwards, giving the impression that the magician has been squashed into virtually nothing – he'd be a big squashed block of meat with a head if the trick was performed for real. Again, this is a great magician's prop, which perfectly disguises the actual location of the magician's body.

As the magician enters the box we see his green shoes sticking out from the two holes at the bottom of the apparatus. These are duplicate feet, kicked into place, sticking out of the front of the box at the bottom. We see the magician's head at the top so we assume that the magician is standing upright. In fact, he is already in position supporting himself in the top half of the box. As the bottom half is compressed upwards the magician puts his hands inside the fake feet so he can make them tap in time with the music. The end result is the magician pretty much on all fours, with the patterns on the box designed to mask the overall size of the top section. This audition appears to be extremely heavily edited and does not show the moments where the magician climbs in and out of the box, so the effect looks really convincing. The judges loved the audition and Michael made it to the next stage.

Michael Late – Semi Final

www.youtube.com/watch?v=Et5TfHDVQ4o

The legacy of the Las Vegas magician Lance Burton cannot be overstated. Again, a Lance Burton routine appears to have been appropriated by another magician and is performed in a similar way but without the beauty of the original performance. When

Lance Burton performed this routine as the "Things Go Bump" illusion he provided context and meaning to the presentation by explaining the story of Indian Shamans. Lance's magic was his tribute to the kind of magic that he believes the Shamans performed. Without the luxury of time, Michael's performance didn't have a narrative. This was compounded by the continuing theme of silliness that was introduced in the audition act. I'm all for silly, silly is fun, but in this performance silly lead to big fake beards that I felt gave the game away.

In Lance Burton's version of this trick, an Indian Tepee stands in the centre of the stage and Lance, donning full Indian headdress, shakes maracas towards an Indian God in the sky. The Tepee is empty, save for the central pole that supports the height of the structure. The Tepee is built onto a platform so the audience can see underneath.

In Michael's act, the headdress is replaced with a hat and silly long flowing fake beard. The tent becomes a wooden hut on wheels, but both performances are basically the same trick and continue in the same way.

Lance raises a curtain in front of the Tepee and Michael raises a tablecloth in front of the hut. The curtain is lowered and there appears to be something moving underneath it. The curtain is dropped completely and whatever it is moves slowly towards the front of the stage. This is repeated until there are four of these unusual things on stage. The curtains are thrown off one at a time to reveal that these strange moving lumps are the magician's assistants, but the real mystery is not revealed until the very end of the act. As the magician walks towards the Tepee / Hut they can be clearly seen shutting themselves inside. Within seconds the final assistant throws off their curtain and we are amazed that the magician was under the last curtain. But, if the magician is one of the moving lumps, he was clearly at the front of the stage under the curtain whilst also on stage before the he entered the Tepee / Hut. How can this possibly have happened? Yet again we see an instant transformation. As an audience we cannot work out how he got from the Tepee to under the curtain. In Michael's version the routine is exactly the same, with his exit into the hut followed by the appearance under the tablecloth.

This trick is beautiful, but again it suffers from the same problem as Chloe's motorbike trick described earlier. In this age of Hard Drive Video Recorders, it's too easy to forget how impressed you were by the trick on the first viewing because it's so easy to instantly rewind and watch again. Like the multiple-out card trick described at the beginning of the book one performance a mystery, but a second performance reduces the routine to puzzle solving and a third viewing tells you everything you need to know.

What I appreciated about Lance Burton's version of this performance was the explanation of the Indian Sharman magicians at the beginning. It provided context, it provided a structure, it provided a great piece of set design, but most importantly it provided justification for Lance to wear an Indian headdress that obscured enough of his face for the routine to work. Michael ran onto the stage and put a hat and huge fake beard on for no real reason, and I feel this would leap out in the mind of the audience, even if they were not familiar with the methods used.

The Tepee and hut seem to follow the same basic magical principle and it's all based on the supporting pole in the centre of the structure. Attached to the pole is a mirror at a 45 degree angle. This means that as far as the audience is concerned the building is empty. In fact, the right hand side of the structure is simply a mirror, reflecting the empty left hand side. We cannot see behind the mirror, and this could be a secret compartment with the assistants hidden inside, or there could be a doorway with the assistants hiding outside at the back on the platform. Either way, the assistants would be clearly visible save for the mirror which hides them from view and creates the illusion of an empty space.

The Tepee / Hut is obscured from view by the curtain / tablecloth and the first assistant comes out from behind the mirror and steps down to the floor and crouches. The cloth is draped over them and they shuffle towards the front of the stage. The magician deliberately hides the entire doorway and also themselves as they lift the curtain, and this is important to provide a consistent appearance. We see the curtain is raised, we see the strange moving lump appear under the curtain and we see the lump move slowly towards the front of the stage. We assume this is the only aspect to the trick, and we see the same movements performed again and again, until there are three assistants produced on stage. For the final time, the magician lifts the curtain in exactly the same way. By now, we've seen it all before and we think we know what is going to happen. Our guard is dropped and the magician knows this and takes advantage. The final assistant steps out of the hiding place, but this one is dressed in the same outfit as the magician. The assistant remains standing and the magician drops down under the curtain. The Indian Headdress disguises this switch perfectly as the magician shuffles away under the curtain, where the lookalike continues to act as if they are the magician. In the Lance Burton routine this really works brilliantly with the Indian dancing in-keeping with the theme of the rest of the routine, but in Michael's version the silly beard doesn't have the same impact and it did look to me that something funny was going on during the switch. Whether you spotted it or not, the lookalike now heads back into the Tepee / hut and the magician is free to whisk off the curtain to thunderous applause.

This was a fun presentation and the judges loved it, but sadly Michael didn't make it to the final.

Jamie Raven – Audition

www.youtube.com/watch?v=f0m9QtYWTIE

Jamie Raven is arguably the magician who has been the most successful since doing so well on Britain's Got Talent, and his career has gone from strength to strength. It's funny that by a magician's standards the tricks he used were very simple, including a trick deck that can be purchased cheaply and performed with very little practice. However the audience loved it and there is a definite lesson that magicians can learn from this performance – again, personality and presentation is the secret to making an audience love your work.

I've seen magicians who perform incredible feats of dexterity when performing card tricks. I would recommend searching YouTube for the work of two incredible performers, Dan and Dave, who have created a number of DVDs of their work as instructional pieces for magicians. I purchased their DVD set "The Trilogy" at a magic convention and was blown away by the complexity of their card flourishes. They would take a lot of time for me to learn but I would be able to impress my magician friends with my new talents if I put the effort in. I've spent time discussing this kind of skill with other magicians and at conventions these performers often try to outdo each other with ever increasing demonstrations of their abilities.

A few years ago I was asked to perform magic at a street market and the organisers told me they would pay for me to do card magic at one of the stalls, but I would also be allowed to sell magic too. This was a win/win to be paid to sell so I went online and purchased two hundred packs of my favourite trick cards. Known as the Svengali deck this is a well known trick and is often found in magic sets aimed at children. In this gimmicked deck the cards alternate and if you spread the deck across the table you can see the first card is a six of hearts, and every alternate card in the deck is an identical six of hearts. The other cards (in the even numbered positions) are all different cards. Each of the sixes are slightly shorter than the different cards so as you handle the deck it is impossible to grip the sixes with your fingers and thumbs. Therefore if you cut the pack, you will grip an indifferent card and the card you cut to will be one of the sixes. If you riffle through the cards and ask the spectator to say stop, they will always stop you on a six. You can show the spectators chosen card going into the middle of the deck, snap your fingers and it will have mysteriously jumped to the top. You can read the spectators mind, "I think your card was the… six of hearts?", or make their card appear in a high up location (by sticking a duplicate six somewhere no-one will see until you point it out). If you riffle through the cards, as your fingers only grip the different cards you will see all the indifferent cards flash past your eyes. However if you riffle from the back of the deck to the front you will only see the sixes and it looks like all the cards magically changed in front of your eyes. If you want to play with magic for the first time, I cannot recommend any trick more than a Svengali deck and it will be the best fiver you ever spend.

Invented in 1908 the Svengali deck is a classic of magic, and I felt this would work against me when demonstrating magic in the market because I bought my first Svengali deck in about 1982 and assumed everyone has seen them by now. I grew up loving magic and the Svengali deck is about as simple, basic and well know as magic comes. With this in mind, I was surprised at how well my demonstrations went at the market and I sold out quickly. Two hundred packets at a fiver each was the easiest thousand pounds I ever earned.

As a working magician it is easy to get sucked into the magic theory and the complex secrets. The incredible work of Dan and Dave is the polar opposite of the self-working trick deck but to the eyes of a spectator the miracle is just as real.

Some elements of the magic world have become dated. Consider for example the hypnotist on TV's Little Britain ("look into the eyes, not around the eyes, but into the eyes"), or the spoof magician Tony LeMesmer from the Alan Partridge chat show, Knowing Me, Knowing You. These characters poke fun at the traditional magician's top hat and tails, and the air of mystery that surrounds them. We all know it's a trick, an elaborate prop or hidden lever, it's not really magic but these performers attempt to wow the audience with their insistence that they really can do incredible things. Whether showing a hugely impressive card flourish (check out Dan and Dave, their stuff is incredible), or filling the studio with dry-ice smoke and telling the audience that "if the trick goes wrong (dramatic pause...) **I could DIE!**" when we know that health and safety legislation wouldn't allow an act like that on TV, magicians have often underestimated the value of simple presentation. Jamie Raven seems to nail this by getting the best reaction of any audience of the previous eight years, and yet the routines being performed are comparatively simple compared to the large scale stage illusions of the other series. What Jamie brings to the table is a fresh, likeable personality. He's not saying "look at me, I can do something you can't do, I am the best magician", he's just a genuine, personable guy showing us some pretty impressive effects. It works in his favour and I'd recommend that any magician learn from this. If you spend your life learning hundreds of incredible tricks and fancy moves, I'd say pick about five of your favourites, and learn how to demonstrate those tricks in a friendly comfortable way. And sell that dry-ice machine, you don't need it.

Jamie approaches the judges, asking for permission to do so. This is really important – he's offering to share his magic with us, not telling us that we are about to see some magic whether we want to or not. This makes a massive impact on the judges who allow him in to their space to see what he will do. Table hopping magicians in restaurants should learn from this.

At first he produces a banknote, and folds it up. It turns into a Britain's Got Talent banknote with images of the judges on. He then follows this up by taking a wad of banknotes and turning them all into the BGT note in the blink of an eye. Finally Jamie uses a deck of cards with a stick man drawn on the back of each card. A random card name is chosen and Jamie then flicks through the cards to show that the stick man is actually part of an animation, like the old flick books you used to play with as a child. By flicking through the cards we see the animated stick man removes his hat, reaches inside and reveals the chosen card.

As mentioned, the theory behind these tricks is considered to be fairly basic among magicians. The tricks with the banknotes are variations of a trick I have performed using lottery tickets where Jamie uses customised BGT banknotes.

In the first part of the audition Jamie shows a £50 note. Hidden behind this is the folded BGT note, held in place by the thumb. The trick involves the bank note being shown on both sides, then folded to match the BGT note in size, with the real money in front of the fake money. Before folding, Jamie demonstrates a great example of sleight of hand by apparently showing both sides of the banknote. This is achieved by folding the banknote in half with the folded side towards the audience. In one smooth motion the other half of the note is unfolded from the back of the note. And the audience has the impression that they saw the note from both sides. In fact the hidden BGT note was always obscured from view by the real banknote.

The £50 note is folded across premade fold scores so it ends up exactly the same size as the hidden note. Jamie blows on the note whilst turning it over so the hidden BGT note is now at the front. He can then unfold the BGT note by reversing the same actions that were used to fold the £50. The end result is that the notes have changed places, and the real money can be hidden in the palm of the hand whilst passing the BGT note to Simon. The next part of the trick involves the wad of money which is stored in the magician's pocket, so as Jamie reaches in to get the money needed for the next trick, the £50 note is dumped in the pocket and the magician is clean, ready to begin the next part of the routine.

For the second trick, Jamie has a wad of banknotes and these instantly transform into more BGT notes to be given to the rest of the judges. There is a wonderful version of this trick that can be bought from magic dealers, called Extreme Burn 2.0 by magic inventor Richard Sanders. I use a less impressive version that is homemade, and you can make this yourself although I would recommend Richard Sanders product which I will not reveal here, suffice to say – it's better!

For my method you need five lottery ticket slips. These can be taken from most newsagents for free without too much suspicion. You also need five twenty pound notes. Lottery tickets are great to use for this trick because they are the same width as a £20 note. You need to line up the lottery tickets with the banknote and trim them with scissors, leaving you with five identical sized lottery tickets, all the same size as a £20 note.

The trick is created by using a gimmick that is made by folding a bank note almost in half, with about 2 centimetres remaining overhanging. A lotto ticket is attached to the banknote at the fold with double sided tape or glue. The lotto ticket is also folded with a 2cm overhang and the finished product is a gimmick that is a Z shape. When folded the gimmick looks like s £20 note, but when turned over it looks like a lotto ticket. I call this a "Z-Gimmick". The gimmick is folded up and the remaining cash is hidden within. The lotto tickets are place on top, with the last one placed underneath. The impression is that there are five lotto tickets but the second from bottom is our gimmick and the cash.

An optical illusion is created in the handling of the lotto tickets. One ticket is passed from the pile to the other hand and then both hands are turned over to show the other sides. A second ticket is passed and the same move takes place which shows us the back of the second ticket in one hand and the same back we saw earlier in the other. The audience believes that they have seen the back of all the tickets, yet the reality is they saw the same ticket from the bottom of the pile each time, and they didn't see the gimmick at all.

The bottom ticket is placed at the top of the pile, leaving the gimmick and the cash at the bottom of the pile, the fingers grip the overhang of the folded gimmick and the whole pile is quickly turned over with a snap. This reverses the situation and the lotto tickets are now hidden by the money. One of the banknotes is taken from the top of the pile and placed on the bottom, which allows the same optical illusion move to be performed, showing the front and back of each banknote. Again, the hand that holds the pile is always showing the back of the bottom bank note, which is important as the audience must not see the gimmick or folded lotto tickets.

There's a simple video on YouTube that explains the process: www.youtube.com/watch?v=PB5yHnfgvts

I would recommend this as a better explanation. The guy who made this video also recommends Extreme Burn 2.0 as a better method.

For the finale to Jamie's audition, he produces the packet of cards and tells the audience that he has drawn the images on the cards himself. He may have done but this is the hardest way, as these packs can be cheaply bought online. I believe the original trick to be called "Card-toon" although there are cheap copies made and sold online. It's worth a few quid to get one of these decks to have a play but any serious magician should stick to a reputable magic dealer and buy the real thing – often the quality of the card stock is considerably higher than in the copy product and this trick involves a lot of wear and tear on the cards so a cheap deck is false economy if you will perform many times.

The deck features a two sided design. At one end of the back of each card there is a frame of the animation of the stick man removing his hat and revealing the card. The last card in the deck is the very last frame before the stick man reveals the card. The selected card is not visible in any frame of this animation.

On the back of each card on the other end is the final frame of animation for the card. For example, if you spread through the deck to locate the seven of clubs, the back of that card would have the stickman holding the seven of clubs on one end of the card and whatever frame of animation in the sequence on the other end. The beauty of this trick is that when you flick through the deck to show the animation, your hand is gripping the other end of the cards, obscuring the secret half of the design and focusing the attention of the audience on the animation half. However the method means that to perform this trick you need to get the chosen card to the bottom of the deck, rotated 180 degrees so the last frame of the animation shows the judge's selected card choice. This was not shown in the TV broadcast and I believe this was to the overall detriment of the effect. Taking the TV broadcast at face value, Simon named a card and Jamie did not touch the deck at any time other than to riffle through and show the animation. In real life he would have needed to show the cards face up, and use a magical method to get the required card to the bottom of the deck in a way that would arouse any suspicion from the audience. Even if he got lucky and the named card happened to be on the bottom already he would still have to have rotated it so the last visible frame of the animation showed the chosen card. So we can only imagine what happened off camera, suffice to say that the chosen card was on the bottom of the deck and this adds the last frame of animation, allowing the stickman to show the card.

Jamie Raven – Semi Final

www.youtube.com/watch?v=qVPp_4Vykbg

This small to large scale illusion was very brave to pull off in the semi final, but for me it has every hallmark of the things hate about magic, so we'll look into this one in detail and together we will try to understand why I didn't like this trick at all.

Jamie shows the judges that he has a deck of cards, each with a word written on. These are apparently just regular random words, the names of objects, written by the audience before the show began. Jamie flicks through the pack from top to bottom, and requests Alicia to say "stop!" at a random point of her choosing. She does so and the cards are cut, apparently at the point that Alicia chose. This may appear to be a free choice but it isn't at all - this is a great example of a card force. The magician could be holding a break in the deck with their little finger (known as a pinkie break as discussed in the Brynolf and Ljung explanation). When Alicia says stop the top half of the cards are removed from the break, not the point where Alicia chose. This brings the cards the magician needs to the top of the deck and what looks like a free choice of four random objects becomes the four objects of the magician's choice.

These four cards are revealed to be Goldfish, Ice, Shoe and Helicopter. One by one, Jamie makes the items appear is if by magic and it was during the first of these that I started to roll my eyes somewhat. As an audience, we are supposed to believe that these items could literally be anything at all – the audience apparently wrote these words at random before the show began. Upon hearing that the first item is a goldfish, Jamie asks a stagehand for a glass of water. We assume that if the card had said a Lion, he'd be asking for a zookeeper. But no, this card says goldfish, and there just happens to be someone at hand with a glass of water. As you read this, turn to the person nearest to you and ask for a glass of water and see how long it takes to come. This trick is already nonsense.

The trick also demonstrated the epic failure of a technique I have used in my own act to varying degrees of success. There is a psychological effect that can work well by referring to something you forced as if it was a random thought. Let's imagine that you have a packet of cards with all of them identical (or maybe use a Svengali deck as explained earlier where you can force the six of hearts). You get a volunteer out of the audience and give them an apparent free choice of card (secretly knowing they will get the six of hearts). Now you get another volunteer out of the audience and do the same thing, forcing a six of hearts on them also.

At this stage we could make a magic effect of the fact they both picked the same card, but let's use a little bit of magical thinking and take this trick further. We ask the first volunteer to **think of their card** – keep it clear and vivid in their mind. We then take the second volunteer and hand them a marker pen and whiteboard. We ask them to look directly at the other volunteer and tune into their wavelength (which means nothing but hey, that's showmanship). Then we ask them to draw their card on the whiteboard, and we keep reinforcing the first volunteer to keep thinking of **the card they are thinking of.**

For every individual in the audience that watches each little movement, burning the magician with their eyes, there's a whole crowd watching that are not paying as much attention.

It's a subtlety but by referring to the card as the card she is **thinking of**, and not the card she chose, the act slowly starts to appear as a mind reading presentation. The audience forgets that we got them to choose a card and might have forced it. The more we talk of the card the volunteer **has in their mind** the more we reinforce they could be thinking of anything at all.

We take the whiteboard from the second volunteer and ask the audience for a round of applause as she takes her seat. Now there is just the magician and the first volunteer on the stage. We reinforce that they are thinking of a specific card, but this could be any card. For the first time, they tell us what card they are thinking of. We show the audience the whiteboard and they go wild. They read each other's minds! This is real magic!

It's not of course, but by steering away from using phrases such as "the card you chose", or "the card I gave you", and instead saying "whatever you are thinking of" you can create the illusion that the spectator could have been thinking of anything. This fails spectacularly in the Britain's Got Talent performance where each judge questions what they are supposed to be doing. Rather than adding a slight confusion to the audience who will misremember what they saw, this approach adds confusion for the judges and they query what they should say next. "Do you mean what am I thinking of, or what's on the card?" asks David Walliams, and similar confusion threatens to spoil the act as each judge queries this use of language. If this was me, as soon as the first judge queried this, I would drop that aspect of the presentation and ask the other judges to name what is written on the cards.

With a glass of water being poured instantly for Jamie (how lucky that there was a stagehand with a glass of water. Good job the card said goldfish!), he holds the glass in full view of the audience and magically makes a goldfish appear. Of course, this is a pre-prepared trick glass with a mirror in one half, similar to the Tepee in Lance Burton's trick discussed earlier. You can see the front half of the glass and the mirror inside gives the illusion that the glass is empty, but the goldfish is hidden behind the mirror. All the magician needs to do is rotate the glass 180 degrees and the goldfish magically appears from nowhere.

As the trick continues another of my bugbears of magic is seen. Jamie is obviously pressed for time in this performance, but even so Jamie appears to have forgotten that the audience believe that the cards were randomly chosen. Jamie should not know what is written on the cards until the judge tells him so. However, he starts to set up the next part of the reveal before being told what the item is. He sets up a lighter and pulls out a piece of flash paper and asks the judge what they are thinking of. What is written on the card is "ice" and this is very lucky as the magician has a block of ice in his pocket. As with all the other uses of Flash paper discussed in this book, the flash conceals the bigger movement, and Jamie simply takes the block of ice in one hand whilst using the distraction of the flash in the other hand.

I would assume that if there was more time, Jamie would have asked the judge what was written on the card, then acted the role, pondering how he could create ice using magic. In this performance he starts the setup before being told what is written on the card, thus proving to the audience that he knows what is written on the cards in advance. I believe this makes the audience question that these are not just random words on cards but ones the magician has put there himself and forced upon the judges, giving away the secret and showing that it's not magic.

To make the next prediction, Jamie reveals his shoe by taking it from his inside jacket pocket. He then points out that his shoe is no longer on his foot. But was it ever on his foot? Did we look at his feet at any point in this performance? Do we care?

This all leads up to the final, and I was really excited at this point because I'd just got a high score on Yahtzee on my iPhone. I know I should have been paying more attention but after the goldfish I really couldn't give a damn about the other stuff.

Amanda Holden can't wait to see how he's going to make a helicopter appear. I hope her reaction to this was genuine, but it's hard to imagine that throughout the rehearsals and all through the filming no-one saw the helicopter being delivered to the studios. Ultimately the helicopter is placed at the rear of the stage and concealed with black backgrounds, no lighting and maybe even a black curtain in front. With the lights down, all it takes is for the spot to be obscured from view by the large white barrier that the magician uses. As soon as the barrier is lifted, any hidden black curtain is removed, the lights come on, the sound effects play and the white barrier is dropped to reveal the helicopter.

I have been harsh in my criticism of this performance, but in honesty, did anyone think this was good? After the low key audition which had been so fantastic, this was a complete change of tack and for me it just didn't work. Maybe they crammed too much in, but the idea that the magician could just conjure up any random item that the audience could name was simply ludicrous and unbelievable. How lucky that there was a glass of water instantly to hand. How lucky that the card said ice, after Jamie had already set up his equipment to make fire that turns into ice. How lucky he had one of his shoes in his pocket. And how exceptionally lucky it was that the last item was the biggest of all, a real show stopper. I went back to my

Yahtzee. The viewers however voted him through to the final. So what do I know?

Jamie Raven - Final

www.youtube.com/watch?v=i7GuwLy41t0

For the final, I was pleased to see Jamie return to the type of magic I really enjoy – close-up. Jamie asked Simon to name any card, and Simon chose the seven of diamonds. Jamie took a deck of cards from his pocket and showed that there was one card that was turned face down in the deck. Sure enough this was the card that Simon had named.

Again we see a really nice performance of what is a simple packet trick that is available from magic dealers. The Invisible deck uses a technique called "Rough and Smooth". The deck can be made at home using a product called roughing fluid, but it can be harmful to breathe the vapours and is not worth the hassle when you can buy a pre-made pack for little money.

The Rough and Smooth fluid is sprayed onto the cards and it dries to form a transparent layer that has a rough gripping texture. If you spray two cards with fluid and leave them to dry they can be placed one on top of the other and this pair of cards will stick together and can be handled as if they are only one card. The rough surface only sticks to other roughed surfaces and this can be used to make miracles happen. During the manufacture of the invisible deck the back of each card is covered in the roughing fluid, and the cards are paired up back to back. This means that if the cards are fanned through the pairs stick together. Each pair has its "mate" on the back side of the pair (the ace of clubs is back to back with the ace of spades for example). If the cards are removed from the box facing up you will see the clubs in order from ace to king, followed by the diamonds. If you remove the pack facing the other way up, you'd see the hearts and spades in the same order.

The spectator gets to name any card, so let's assume they chose the seven of spades. The magician takes the deck of cards and rotates it so that when the cards are removed from the box the club/diamond side is face up. The magician fans through the cards showing all the cards are face up which is easy because the face down cards are all on the other side of each card stuck with the roughing fluid. When the magician gets to the mate (the seven of clubs) he loosens his grip on the pair, and the face up card slides across leaving the face down card visible, The deck looks like there is only one card face up, and of course this is the spectator's choice.

For the next part of the routine, Jamie uses magical thinking to combine one of his earlier tricks with a new one, again making something bigger. Earlier he gave Alicia a present, asking her not to open it. He now takes one of the Britain's Got Talent bank notes from the previous performance and asks Alicia to sign it so that it cannot be switched with a duplicate note later. Jamie then folds up the signed note and repeats the same changeover as in his audition, but instead of making it change to real money it changes to a note that says "look inside the box".

Inside the box is another box. Inside that box is a red bag. Inside that bag is a lemon. It's important that Jamie does not allow Alicia to open the bag herself and she passes it to Jamie who shows his right hand is empty, reaches into the bag and (after a little fumbling... what could be going on there?) he pulls out the lemon. Taking a knife from his pocket he cuts the lemon in half and we see the signed BGT banknote folded neatly inside the lemon.

This trick was widely criticised on Twitter by eagle eyed viewers posting photographs of an unfortunate camera angle that appeared to show that the banknote was obscuring the hole in the end of the lemon that was used to slide the note into place. As the note was removed from the lemon you could just about see the light from the other side, showing that the lemon was tucked into a hole that lead all the way outside of the fruit. This is a shame because the trick is a really good trick, but as discussed earlier in the Doug Henning/Chloe Carter explanation, TV magic can really suffer in the world of PVRs and TV that lets you rewind and freeze-frame instantly.

This brings us to the end of series nine, and a very successful year for magic on Britain's Got Talent. The success of magic was to continue right through to the present, with the first winner in series ten, and loads more magic to come in the final two series.

Series 10 – 2016

And so, we arrive at series ten, and finally we get a series winner, Richard Jones. The patriotic combination of army hero and magician, Richard seemed to walk through the whole competition and finally completely validate the position of magician on Britain's Got Talent. The next series would have more magic than any other to date, thanks largely to Richard Jones proving that magic can win this competition. But first...

Christian Lee – Audition

www.youtube.com/watch?v=pm-NLCYK9WI

Setting the comedy standard for what was to follow, Christian confidently walked out onto the stage, removed his sunglasses to reveal another pair behind them, then inflated a washing up glove, which changed into a bottle of champagne when burst. The bottle is carried in the inside left of his jacket, and gripped by the cork end in the magician's hand before turning the hand to make the bottle rotate forward. This brings the bottle into view as the distraction of the burst rubber distracts the eye. Magicians use a large inside pocket sewn into the inside of the jacket (known as a Topit), to hold the bottle in place, and specific gimmicks for this exact trick can be purchased from magic dealers. Made from plastic, these bottle holders can connect to the trouser belt, obscured from view by the flap of the jacket.

There's not a lot to explain the remainder of this audition, but it's a fantastic lesson in magical thinking. At the heart of the routine is the same trick we saw earlier, known as the invisible deck as performed by Jamie Raven in the previous series. However, rather than ask the volunteer to name a card, then have the magician find it upside down in the deck, Christian makes the focus of the routine about the comedy. Christian inflates a huge red balloon and stretches it over his head. He swings the balloon to tap Amanda on the forehead as if to implant a magical card suggestion into her mind. When the balloon is removed from his head he uses the jet of escaping air to recreate the famous flying scene from the movie Titanic, complete with the Celine Dion music. It's hilarious and gets a great reaction.

The trick becomes secondary to the comedy and it is this that elevates the presentation to something magical, memorable and fun. The use of a huge red balloon as some kind of mind-magic device works brilliantly and this is once again something all magicians can learn from. The trick does not require any sleight of hand or special magic skills, but hinges of the showmanship, personality and fun that the magician brings to the table. Christian sailed through to the semi finals, with great judge's comments. Once again, Simon hit the nail on the head by explaining that he wasn't overly impressed by the magic on display but really enjoyed the act overall. By combining comedy with magic, Christian got a 'yes' vote from Simon, even though Simon didn't enjoy the magic.

Christian has also become well known to those who didn't see the show as a clip of this routine went viral over social media. A cheeky little trick at the end had his unravelling a hidden bra from his hand, so as Amanda walked away from him it looked like he had somehow unhooked it and pulled it away from her. The YouTube clip, titled "Magician steals Amanda's Bra!" has been seen hundreds of thousands of times. In a competitive world, it's great to see a magician gaining exposure so widely thanks to the internet.

Christian Lee – Semi Final

www.youtube.com/watch?v=JjdR80Es6sE

For the semi final, Christian asked David Walliams to join him on stage and offered him an apparent free choice of card from the deck. The card is signed and returned to the deck. The magician is, as always, going to locate the card, or make it appear somewhere, we've seen it before. Again, Christian takes this routine to a different level, with clever and fun presentation of what is ostensibly a standard piece of magic. Misdirection is also used in the form of an alternate ending to the routine that an experienced magician would be expecting. The use of a "card-sword" makes anyone familiar with magic expect to see the signed card appear on the end of the sword, but Christian gives David his wallet which adds an unexpected twist to the routine.

The signed card is replaced into the pack, and during the discussion with David (and the audio clip of Little-Mix, combined with a distant camera shot) the chosen card is shuffled to the top of the deck, then palmed into the pocket at the same time as the magician fumbles for the Japanese head band.

As the card is secreted into the pocket, it is placed inside the wallet. This would be difficult, especially as the card is a zipped compartment inside the wallet, but luckily magic dealers make wallets specifically for this purpose. Known as "card to wallet", my choice is manufactured by a dealer called Propdog, and was designed by Jerry O'Connell. The Jerry O'Connell Wallet has a hidden slot on the outside of the wallet which leads to the inside zipped pocket. The card is slipped into the slot very quickly and easily, and the quality of the O'Connell wallet makes this simple. Other dealers sell different variations of the card to wallet, and I would recommend Alakazam Magic, Harry Robson Magic or Propdog as good dealers with a range of wallets to explore should you wish to buy one. Some wallets take the idea further, and, as in this performance, add other trick methods to enhance the effect. In this case not only does the card appear in the wallet, but inside an envelope that was in the wallet! This effect can be achieved by using a gimmicked envelope inside the trick wallet. The end of the envelope could be cut away so the card slides inside the envelope as it slides into the wallet. Magicians use special glue which is known as Blue-Glue (also called repositional glue – I use one by a brand called Zig which is applied from a chisel tip like a marker pen). Blue Glue works like regular glue for sticking paper together, but if the glue is applied and then left without any other surface being attached, the glue dries to a transparent, tacky finish. When paper is pushed against the glue later, it sticks immediately. This means the envelope can be placed into the wallet with the open end wedged, awaiting the chosen card to be slipped inside. As the envelope is removed from the wallet, a firm press on the outside pushes the tacky side against the other envelope wall and the envelope appears sealed from all sides.

As a great distraction to the wallet, Christian brings out the Japanese headbands and explains that he has a sword at his side. This is another prop available from magic dealers. The card sword allows a card to be hidden in the handle and by pressing a button the card appears as if from nowhere, impaled on the tip of the sword. By using this prop, I forgot about the wallet assuming he would spike the chosen card whilst balancing on the unicycle. Again, magical thinking tells us that an audience of laypeople would be impressed at the ability to impale *any* card whilst balanced on a unicycle, so this still impresses, even though it's not the correct card. However the card is revealed in an envelope inside the wallet instead and this is a great ending to a great Semi Final. Sadly this was the last we saw of Christian as he did not make to the final.

Richard Jones – Audition

www.youtube.com/watch?v=pHfBXQ5CL0Y

Richard Jones' audition used magic and mind reading to impress and he explains in his introduction that what fascinates him is not the magic itself but the reaction seen in the faces of the audience. I agree with this completely. The magic happens in the mind of the spectator.

Richard begins by joining the judges and handing a shiny bag containing a gift to Simon. He produces two notebooks and flicks through the pages to reveal that each page has writing on. In the first book every page has the name of a celebrity, and the second book has a drink on each page. Amanda and David are asked to take a pad each and they hold it, sandwiched between their hands for safe keeping.

The judges are then asked to open the pads at a random page each, look inside, then slam the pads shut and throw them onto the stage. In doing so, Amanda now has the name of a celebrity chosen from all those we saw written in the book, and David has a drink selected from the many sodas and cocktails we saw earlier. By flicking through the pages of the pads, these choices appear random. But are they?

Earlier in the book we discussed the Svengali deck, a trick pack of cards that creates the illusion of a full pack, whilst ensuring that a volunteer does not get a free choice of card. In my Svengali decks every other card in the deck is a six of hearts, and these cards are slightly shorter than the alternating different cards. When you flick through the deck from the front to the back, two cards fall as one every time so the spectator only ever sees the different cards, with the sixes hidden behind as each pair falls. If the cards are flicked back to front the same thing happens, with the spectator only seeing the six of hearts.

If the spectator cuts the deck, the top card that they cut to will always be the six of hearts, even though it appears that they had a free choice of any of the cards they saw. The Svengali Pad works in the same way with alternate pages of the pad slightly shorter than the other pages. When the pad is flicked through from the top to the bottom you only see the even numbered pages as they fall in pairs. The unnatural element to this trick that shows Svengali Pads are being used comes from the way the magician asks the judges to hold the pad sandwiched between their hands. This is not a normal way to hold a pad! In doing this, the judges are placed in a position that will force them to open the pad when instructed to by lifting the page in the same way you would do so when flicking the pad from bottom to top. In the same way that every alternate card in a Svengali deck is the six of hearts, every alternate page in the Svengali Pad says David Beckham.

Again, magical thinking comes into play, because it would be easy for the magician to simply ask, "Are you thinking of David Beckham?" to prove he could read Amanda's mind. To make this more impressive (and to add further distance between the use of the pads and the actual mind read), Richard claims to have spent six years studying Origami in Japan, and if that's true, I will eat my hat, my shoes and maybe my trousers. He takes a piece of paper and starts to snip away at sections with scissors. By performing a switch, similar to Jamie Raven's tricks involving bank notes from the previous year, the piece of snipped paper is swapped to a piece with an elaborately cut out image of David Beckham which looks far too perfect to have been done live with a clunky pair of scissors. I'm sure these are made using computers, specialist cutting tools and stencils.

To follow this up, Richard reveals his other prediction by asking David Walliams which drink he was thinking of. David was thinking of a cup of tea and Richard reaches into the bag to reveal... a can of fizzy orange soda. We know from the Svengali Pad that David had no choice but to choose a cup of tea and we know that the trick hasn't really gone wrong, but how is the magician going to make the can of orange soda into tea?

It's impossible, as with all the methods in this book to confirm exactly how the performer chooses to do this trick. One method would be to simply buy from a magic dealer a can that is labelled as orange soda but contains tea. This could be boiled in a pan before the performance to make it hot. The reason I feel this could be a prop is that the brand of drink is not one I have heard of. This could also be because of TV rules regarding product placement (the TV company might have had to blur out the brand if they had used, say, a Coca Cola can for example), or it could be because a dealer manufactures a trick can but does not have the rights to reproduce the logo.

My method would be to make the prop yourself. I favour the second method as all the gimmicks I know of to put things into sealed cans have been demonstrated to me using objects, not liquids (Google for a trick called Deceptus, by inventor Jimmy Strange to see what I mean). However, a good friend of mine came up with a method that would work, by scanning the barcode from a can into his computer and printing sticky labels on his home printer. He would produce sheets of these labels using PowerPoint on the computer, meticulously designed to match the dimensions of the barcode on a 33ml can of soda. The labels were bought from a specific supplier that makes waterproof labels.

To prepare for this trick, I would brew up a nice pot of tea and whilst it was cooling down I would take a branded soda can and hold it over the sink. Then I would pierce the can in the centre of the barcode using a pin. When you do this, the force of the carbonated liquid squirts a jet of soda across the kitchen so you need to be careful. When the soda quirt settles, you can use a nail or any method you deem safe to make the hole bigger, enough to empty out the contents of the can. Using a funnel you fill the can with the cooled tea and cover the hole with a barcode sticker. No-one will question the sticker, especially if you make a good job of keeping it lined up straight.

By boiling water in a pan, the can is rested in the shallow water with the label sticking out of the top. This way the only risk to the labels stability is the steam, and a quality waterproof label will not cause an issue. All you need to do is get the tea warmed to a temperature that convinces the audience the tea is hot. It does not need to be boiling and will stay hot for longer than you might imagine inside the can.

One lovely piece of theatre is that the can is produced from the bag as if the trick has gone wrong. The audience and judges at this point would not assume the can is anything other than room temperature. The magician holds the can as if it is a regular soda can, and before anyone else gets to touch it he starts to make out that he is using his powers to make the can start to become warm. We know it's already warm but the judges do not and they cannot believe the magician is somehow making the can hot in front of their very eyes. They reach to touch the can to check, and as it is hot they believe that it is suddenly becoming hot by magic. The magician uses powerful suggestive language, describing how the can is getting hotter, and the audience believes this.

The method I suggest for making a hot soda can filled with tea is the method I would use, but it is in no way foolproof and I would recommend a bit of magical thinking yourself to come up with a method that is safe and works for you. In my preparation to perform this trick I have burned myself without thinking because a metal can will get incredibly hot! There is a definite risk of injury, and although I can perform this trick without any problems I have got into this position through a great deal of trial and error! I do not take any responsibility if you try this yourself and get hurt, whether that's by hot splashing tea, boiling water or anything else. Rule number one – be careful and stay safe!

Richard Jones – Semi Final

https://www.youtube.com/watch?v=bJ_vf8ljgHU

We discussed at the beginning of this book that a good piece of advice for anyone trying to work out the method to a magic trick is to concentrate of every aspect of what you can see, no matter how trivial or unimportant it may appear. For example, if a magician asks you to choose a page from a book, then to choose a word, then reads your mind to tell you what the word was, could they have done the same trick without the book?

Similarly, if a magician asked you to think of a card, then read your mind to tell you which card it was that would be a miracle. But if the magician takes a deck of cards and asks you to shout stop as he flicks through the deck, you can be sure that this unnatural looking approach to card selection is narrowing your choices, usually to a specific card. If the magician can sit his assistant in a big chair then make her disappear, could he do it without the chair? In magic, the smallest object can contain the biggest secrets, and nowhere is this demonstrated better on BGT than in Richard Jones' semi final act.

Again, Richard gives a present to Simon which stays on the table in full view throughout the performance. Richard then takes a copy of Amanda Holden's autobiography and invites Alicia to shout 'stop!' as he riffles through the pages. Alicia stops on a specific page and is asked to remember the page number and the first word on that page.

Unknown to the audience, this is a forced decision because it doesn't matter where Alicia chooses because Richard is always going to show her the same page number and same first word. The key element to this trick is the use of a photograph of the judges to flick the pages with. There's simply no reason to do that, unless it's something to do with the trick – the magician could easily flick the pages with his fingers and by using the photograph it causes him to hold the book in the air and fold the cover back in an unnatural position. It would appear much cleaner to just flick the pages by hand, but that would stop the trick from working because the entire trick is only possible because of the secret held within that photograph.

The audience does not see the back of the photograph and it's with good reason. Attached to the back of the photograph is the corner piece of one page of Amanda's book. This is the force page that Alicia needs to choose. The photograph is used to flick through the pages of the book and when Alicia chooses to stop the photograph is inserted between the pages. Although this is genuinely a free choice, Richard then peels open the page of the book allowing Alicia to see which page she chose and which word she needs to remember. The corner of the book she can see is not the page that she stopped at but the page that is attached to the back of the photograph. Once Alicia has remembered the page number and word, the trickery is complete and the rest of the performance is presentation.

Inside the bottle is the page that matches the forced page, number 176. Alicia turns to page 176 in the book, but it is no longer there. The reason is because it was never there, and the ripped out page was in the bottle from the start of the trick. Alicia believes that the page she saw has now somehow become ripped out of the book because she believes she saw it just moments ago, but the page she saw was attached to the photograph which is now inside the performer's pocket.

To create a climax to the trick, the page has been prepared with the word "bottom" on the back. The page is lit on fire and then turned around to show the first word on the page that Alicia was asked to memorise earlier. Again, this was from the forced page so the word was always going to be "bottom".

This routine is a great example of taking a small secret and making a much bigger effect. For me, it was an interesting learning experience seeing how a non-magician can misremember the magic to create an effect in their mind that is bigger than the actual effect they saw. When this was first broadcast, my grandmother phoned me up and asked me how it was done. She did not believe my explanation because she had no memory of the photograph of the judges. In her mind she was convinced that the magician handed Alicia the book and she had a completely free choice of page. My Gran had seen with her own eyes Alicia browsing the book, choosing a page, then closing the book and handing it back to the magician. I ended up showing her the clip on YouTube to demonstrate and it was only then that she remembered the photo. Such an innocuous little touch, yet completely vital to the presentation and the trick becomes bigger in the audience's memory because they don't remember the photograph.

Many years ago I was at a Christmas meal with work colleagues and a magician was table-hopping doing card tricks. During that day a customer had misheard my colleague Tammy when she gave her name, and called her Panda throughout the transaction. Tammy's friends had chosen to call her Panda throughout the evening meal as it was making them laugh a lot. When the magician came to the table, he asked Tammy to sign her name on a randomly chosen card. Tammy wrote Panda for fun, and the magician took the card, folded it into four, dropped it in an ashtray and set it on fire (ashtrays in a restaurant really shows how old this story is, doesn't it?). The card then reappeared later stuck to the ceiling. The card was unfolded to reveal the same card with the same signature.

The reason that the card was folded in four was because the magician needed to switch the card before it went into the ashtray. By folding it up you could no longer see the signature or card value, and a random duplicate card was burned. The original card was planted by the magician on the ceiling during the distraction of the groups focus on the ashtray and the magic was complete.

Afterwards, Tammy said to me she had no idea how the trick was done, and was asking for my opinion, which I refused to give as I was enjoying watching her trying to puzzle it out. She knew, 100% that there was a duplicate card because she had seen the card burning in the ashtray. However, in her mind the card that was signed was burned, the duplicate card was on the ceiling. In her mind she understood exactly what was going on, right up until the end moment when the card had her signature on it. When she asked me how that happened, she could not get over the fact that the magician had somehow known that she was calling herself Panda that day, because somehow the magician needed to copy her signature onto that duplicate card. From that revelation, no explanation made any sense to her because in her mind the only secret left to understand was how the magician knew the name Panda – the idea that the card on the ceiling was exactly the same card she signed originally was never in her mind and now, at this late stage, she could never unravel the exact events. Just as my Gran had no memory of Richard Jones' photo, Tammy had a very clear memory of the burning card with her signature on and from that point on she was completely fooled. There was no telling her that it wasn't her card that burned because she saw it with her own eyes!

In a similar way, I performed a series of simple card tricks for a bunch of primary school children using a one way deck (52 cards with all of them being the ten of diamonds). At the end of the trick, I showed them that I was simply being cheeky and demonstrated that all the cards were the same. I expected groans of derision as they realised they had been fooled but it turned out to be a great climax to the routine as the kids were convinced that I had used magic to make all the cards change to be the same. The magic had again created a false memory and the kids thought that I had showed the cards to be all different before I started. I hadn't of course, but I jumped on this opportunity and took the praise for my miracle. I heard them telling their friends later about the incredible magic they had seen!

The magic in a performance happens in the spectators mind, and in recalling the magic the volunteer will often recount to others specific events that simply didn't happen. The spectator recollects memories that were not there and remembers a bigger effect to what really happened. This is worth keeping in mind if you design your own magic act, because as a performer you become so close to the magic that it's easy to forget that what you are doing is not necessarily what the audience is seeing.

Richard Jones – Final

www.youtube.com/watch?v=H6Oh3F6CHDQ

For Richard's final act, a patriotic and moving performance of a brilliantly adapted storytelling trick tugged on the heartstrings of the audience, and lead to Richard winning the whole series overall. Richard is seen to be handling and shuffling a deck of cards but exercising complete control of the deck so that he can tell a story with the cards matching the narrative. Richard tells the heroic story of one of the people who inspired him in magic.

"He was born in 1918, and in 1936 he became a member of the magic circle."

As the story is told, the cards are dealt to the table and the values of the cards mirror the story being told (1918 and 1936 being ace, nine, ace, eight, ace, nine, three, six). During the storytelling routine, Richard performs a torn and restored card trick, tearing the card into four pieces then fusing the pieces back together with a lighter. The trick climaxes with a photograph of the man himself, Fergus Anckorn, spread onto the table, formed from images printed on the cards.

Taking these magic routines and applying context to them makes this collection of three tricks into an emotional and moving performance. To focus on the magic, there are two main skills on display here, the first being card control and the second is the performance of the torn and restored card illusion.

For a stunning example of the storytelling card trick, the magician Bill Malone does a flawless and fast demonstration on one of his instructional DVD sets. Bill's effect, known as "Sam the Bellhop" is as good as it gets, although other variations such as James Galea's "671 King Street", have gone viral on YouTube. The basic premise of each of these routines is the same. The magician tells a story of what happened to him on a night out, spelling the details with the cards, whilst taking every opportunity to shuffle and mix the cards to show that they are not in a predetermined order. Both James Galea and Bill Malone perform many methods of "Fake Shuffling", the idea being to give the impression that the cards are being thoroughly mixed. The audience should see that the cards are mixed up and the magician is somehow controlling the cards he needs to tell the story. The reality is that the cards are in the order needed to tell the story from the start and the magician's shuffles and cuts are cleverly retaining the order so they can continue to tell the story.

For the next effect, Richard takes one of the cards and asks for it to be signed by Amanda to prevent it being switched for another. The card is apparently folded into four, torn around the folds and ripped into separate pieces. You really can see the individual pieces of the card in his hand – that's real ripping you can see. A lighter is taken from the inside of the magician's army uniform and the edges of the card appear to be fused together as the card is unfolded and restored to one piece.

The (extremely) English magician, Guy Hollingworth absolutely blew my mind with this trick when I was very young, and it remains a wonderful piece of magic. I'm sorry to say that I feel the way it was performed on Britain's Got Talent was very basic and quite clumsy. For a perfect demonstration, search for Guy

Hollingworth on YouTube as the torn and restored card is a thing of beauty in his hands.

For a simple torn and restored, I recommend the magicians DVD, "Rehab – Real World Torn and Restored Card". This is available quite cheaply online and I feel it s the best compromise I have seen between ease of performance and impressive looking effect.

In all versions of torn and restored the secret involves the destruction of a duplicate card. The key is to hide the original signed card which is folded behind a duplicate which is then torn into pieces. Often you can see the magician holds the pile of torn pieces in their mouth, with one of the pieces being the original card still folded into four. One of the tricky moves in this kind of routine is to take the pieces together in a pile, and secretly discard the torn pieces to leave the original card, still folded into four (resembling a pile of 4 pieces) in hand whilst the other pieces are somehow ditched. In this performance Richard dumps the pieces inside his jacket as he reaches for the lighter, which is a really nice touch. As discussed earlier his previous trick with Amanda Holden's book, there's no real reason for a photograph of the judges to be used and this masks a bigger secret. In this routine the lighter seems to be used to fuse the pieces back together, but the card in hand is intact all along, and the lighter is a distraction to allow the magician to reach into his jacket to dump the torn pieces.

Finally a really lovely yet incredibly simple effect brings the performance to its climax. The cards are riffle shuffled once more, retaining the bottom nine cards in order. These cards have the photograph of the man who was the inspiration for this whole routine stuck to the backs. The photograph is printed into adhesive paper, cut into nine sections and stuck onto the cards. The surface of the table is enough to make the bottom card stay in place as the deck is slid three times to make three columns. The cards slide from the bottom of the deck one at a time, and the images are in order so that the finished nine card image is complete. You can see that this goes wrong on the night, when two cards stick together. This leaves an extra card in the middle row face down, and Richard has to separate the two stuck cards and ditch the random extra card to make the image.

For me, the atmosphere created by the story, the music and the revelation of Fergus Anckorn (the former soldier and longest serving member of the Magic Circle) made this routine a worthy winning performance, even though the magical content was pretty standard stuff if we're being honest. I prefer Bill Malone's spelling trick, Guy Hollingworth's torn card trick, and the final effect went wrong a bit – but as I keep hammering home (in what some would call tedious detail and repetition), it's not about the secret, or even about the magic. It's about the way your performance makes the audience feel and there are few examples that demonstrate this better that Richard's final act. A worthy winner.

Series 11 – 2017

Finally, we arrive at the current series, at least at the time of writing. Magic has truly been accepted as a viable art and is more popular than ever. With more magicians than in any previous series, there's a lot for us to cover in this final section. Magicians from the UK competed with magic from Holland and Japan to make this, in my opinion, the best series yet.

Tanba – Audition

www.youtube.com/watch?v=PBKA0JlT3Rw

Professional magician Tanba provided an incredible action packed and fast paced performance, and got a great response from the judges, who sadly decided later not to put him through to the final. His numerous effects were performed so quickly it's hard to keep up when watching the performance. As discussed at the beginning of this book, dangerous magic should not be performed at home without the necessary training and skills and I cannot possibly cover all the stunts from this performance in enough detail to cover all the information you would need to know to understand this routine. However, if you would like to learn more, Tomas Medina released a DVD called Geek Magic that covers the detail of swallowing razor blades. Whilst educational magic DVDs are often categorised as "E" (exempt from classification), this one has warnings that it is not for sale to those under eighteen years of age, and anything that involves razor blades is inherently going to be dangerous. Likewise, the balloon swallow trick has been around for many years, and recently a magician named Justin Meitz released a DVD of his method which included a new technique to half swallow the balloon then bring it back out again. The DVD is called "Deep" and can be purchased online, but the key to any balloon swallow is to understand before you even begin that you do not ever swallow the balloon. Choking on a balloon could easily cause death, and all the balloon swallow techniques I have come across involve the illusion of the balloon being swallowed whilst it is actually deflating. However you perform the trick you need to understand that even though you don't really swallow anything, a rubber balloon in the mouth is never a good idea and should that balloon pop you would potentially inhale the balloon while breathing. It's a trick I perform myself but for me it involved a lot of learning before even contemplating giving it a try, and a long conversation with an experienced performer who recommended the best balloons to use to minimise the risk of popping.

Tanba does demonstrate a lovely prop that is a favourite effect of mine, as he pours a drink of Absinthe into a glass. As he pours the drink he lets go of the glass that stays suspended in mid air. This is a commercially available prop from magic dealers and the glass and bottle come together as a set. The magician starts to pour the drink and brings the glass up to the mouth of the bottle. The glass hooks onto a reel which extends a thread down and the glass hangs from the thread. The brightly coloured liquid hides the thread from view. It's a simple trick but it looks great when performed well.

Tanba was an amazing performer but there were a few headlines in the following days as newspapers were critical of a professional magician from Japan appearing on Britain's Got Talent. This seemed unfair criticism to me as many of the performers on these shows are professionals at what they do and if Tanba wants to travel from Japan then he's surely allowed to! However, whether it was the newspapers reaction or some other reason, Tanba did not appear in the semi finals, despite getting through the audition.

Josephine Lee – Audition

www.youtube.com/watch?v=XFZj9u9d7FU

Like Chloe Louise Crawford in series nine, Josephine Lee was a former magician's assistant now performing as the main attraction. I really enjoyed this audition, and it's funny to see how different magicians take on the same ideas and work with them to make something of their own. Earlier we discussed how Michael Late performed a comedy themed performance of "Things Go Bump" which I first saw with a Native American Indian theme performed by Lance Burton. Here, we see Josephine performing a levitating ball illusion that turns into "Things Go Bump", using the levitating balls instead of other assistants.

You'll remember that Lance Burton used a Tepee in the centre of the stage with a hidden mirror obscuring the assistant entry to the stage. Michael Late used a hut to similar effect and in this version Josephine uses a wooden crate. I believe the crate has a hidden flap in the back wall, or, as we have seen earlier with thick tables and platforms, the crate could have a well in the bottom with a hidden assistant. There needs to be someone to load the floating balls onto the mechanism above the stage that the balls float from.

Earlier when discussing cheaply made copy versions of magician's props I discussed the Losander Table. This beautiful piece of magic is the ultimate in levitation effects when performed well. In the Losander illusion the magician is in control of the table as it floats, but we can see from the dance moves that Josephine is not controlling the first ball as it floats in the air, suspended from the ceiling. Josephine beautifully demonstrates the ball is not suspended from the ceiling by using a hoop, in a similar way to Stevie Pink in series seven.

The movement of the hoop suggests that it travels all the way around the floating ball, but closer inspection reveals the wire that holds the ball prevents the hoop from passing above the ball. The hoop can be rotated behind the ball if the audience is not close up as the white coloured ball obscures the part of the hoop that goes in front of the ball. However my favourite technique for this is so cheeky that you'd think audiences would spot it – but they never do! For this, the magician holds the hoop level with the centre of the ball with the top of the hoop almost touching the hidden wire. The hoop is rotated one full turn and the top of the hoop travels from behind the wire, under the ball and comes to a stop in the upright position with the hoop now in front of the wire. The magician immediately rotates the hoop back in the same direction it came. From a distance (and especially with the flat, 2D image on the TV screen) the hoop looks like it continues to turn in the same direction. The magician needs a great deal of practice to perform this smoothly, keeping the speed constant so as not to arouse suspicion from the audience.

Whichever technique is used the theory is the same as when Stevie Pink used a hoop as a convincer in his levitation. The hoop is not rotated around the floating object, but merely passed around the object and the mechanism that keeps it aloft. It really looks like the hoop is rotating multiple times around the ball, convincing the audience that the ball is floating on its own.

The rest of this illusion follows the same principle of the "Things Go Bump" illusion explained earlier. For this method the same elaborate rigging in the ceiling that provides the means of floatation for the first ball also controls the silver curtains that appear to contain shells sewn into them so that they appear to have a ball underneath when suspended from the invisible wires. As you'll recall, a similar technique was used by Brynolf and Ljung to give the illusion that someone was sat in the prop chair when the curtain was draped over them. A secret assistant from the unusually thick table that the crate stands on hides the display ball from view when Josephine lifts the curtain. The curtain is lifted further to cover Josephine's face, a movement will be repeated each time so the final time does not attract suspicion by looking different. The invisible thread is operated from above and the shell in the curtain gives the illusion that the ball is floating as before and taking the curtain away towards the front of the stage. Josephine closes the doors to the front of the box, and the secret assistant places the ball back on the plinth. The process is repeated. Then for the third time, Josephine herself goes under the curtain and the secret assistant leaps from their hiding place. This assistant has blonde hair that matches Josephine's but she messes it up so we cannot see her face. We make out enough for us to believe that the third curtain has another floating ball underneath and the lookalike ducks down into the crate. She drops back into her hiding place, the crate is shown to be empty and the first two curtains are dropped to the floor. Since these do not have anything under them, merely the shell shape sewn into the lining, they drop virtually flat. Finally Josephine reveals that she is under the third curtain and the effect is complete. A really good reworking of the same illusion we saw by Michael Late but with a completely different presentation.

Josephine Lee – Semi Final

www.youtube.com/watch?v=Ndod4DPrpHs

Throughout the course of this book, we have watched and studied a lot of magic together. We've started to see the same magical techniques used in different ways to create new presentations of the same methods. When Josephine Lee walked onto the stage for her semi final performance surrounded by male assistants wearing large hoods, I remember thinking, "I wonder when she's going to switch places with one of them?"

We've already seen the faces of assistants being obscured by hoods, Indian headdresses, crash helmets and fake beards and now we're starting to predict the magic before it has even started!

Perhaps the switch would take place during the large illusion that was set up to the left of the stage. Here, we see a piece of equipment which allows the assistants to chain Josephine in place by wrapping her in chains that follow a Z-shape design. There are loops on both sides of the performer with three loops on one side and two on the other. The chains look like they hold the magician in place firmly, but because of the Z-shape layout of the chain, a secret mechanism allows the side with the 2 loops to come away from the illusion. This makes the chain resemble an open door, allowing the magician to step out and the assistant to step in. By adding a costume quick-change at this point (see the Visage explanation earlier), the magician has swapped places with the assistant, and now has a red dress on – all performed in seconds!

I'm still waiting at this point for Josephine to transform into one of the hooded assistants, and after a table walks across the stage pushed only by a pair of legs (with either the upper half of the assistant's body hidden inside the table, or a more elaborate version with robotic legs - either way it's an impressive and expensive purchase from the magic dealer), Josephine and the assistants walk over to another box on stage.

We've seen a big box on a table a number of times now, and we know that the interior of the box is bigger than it would appear because the box and table are one unit. This trick usually involves the assistant climbing inside then being squashed to one end of the box before revealing it to be completely empty. This illusion was revealed on an episode of The Masked Magician, showing that the assistant slips into the bottom of the box into a hidden compartment within the table. However, for this version, we still predict that Josephine will replace one of the hooded assistants. Yet again, a hidden extra assistant is already in this box and Josephine barely spends a moment in there with her, because as she is lifted into the box by her assistants she drops straight into the hollow steps behind which are immediately wheeled off stage. Josephine dons the hooded costume off-stage while the secret assistant pretends to be Josephine in the box. As the side of the box is compressed to squeeze Josephine apparently to one end of the box, our body double slips below into the hidden compartment. Meanwhile the assistants dance and move around on the stage, with one switching places with Josephine. The magic is complete and as the box is shown to be empty (with the secret assistant hidden in the base), Josephine whisks off the hood and reveals the apparent, instant transformation.

I enjoyed the combination of ideas and effects in this performance and especially liked the twist on the last box illusion, but I found the voice over to be distracting – for me, it seemed to tip the balance of my concentration and when I listened to the words I wasn't paying attention to the magic. When I watched magic, I wasn't listening. The act was well received, but didn't secure Josephine a place in the final.

Niels Harder – Audition

www.youtube.com/watch?v=ahId0ScqzXE

"What the hell?" exclaimed Ant after taking part in this extremely strange performance. For me, the funniest part of his act wasn't from the magician, whose humour didn't really work for me, but from Ant trapped in a guillotine, on all fours, as Niels brought out a cucumber. Ant looked panicked – "Where are you going to stick that?" he trembled.

Niels Harder stormed the stage with an act that I'm sure the audience at home would instantly love or hate. Strutting around the stage like he owned it Niels raised plenty of laughs in the audition and sailed through based on the persona of his performance. In terms of magic alone there was very little to see of any interest. A tube was shown to be empty then a silk handkerchief was produced from it (trick tube, hanky hidden between inner and outer wall) and a piece of rope went stiff on command (trick rope, has a frame inside that only bends one way, making the rope feel loose and floppy when held one way and lays solid when rotated to face upwards). The main performance, which I did find hilarious, I'm just not sure why, involved Ant's head being pushed through a guillotine. The aforementioned cucumbers were slotted through the device, one on each side of Ant's head. The cucumbers were sliced through by the blade of the guillotine but Ant kept his head and safely returned to Dec at the side of the stage who was crying with laughter.

The guillotine itself is another classic piece of magical invention, which originally took the form of the full size equipment used for beheadings but as magicians started to travel from one venue to another the smaller "Head Chopper" illusion was created where the magician thrusts the blade through the frame of the illusion themselves. There are many variations of the method, but they usually involve either a duplicate blade that falls from below the volunteer's neck as the first blade is stopped mechanically and hidden in the wooden frame above the volunteer. Other methods include an L shaped blade that rotates around the volunteer's neck, causing no injury whilst still slicing the cucumbers in the sides. Whichever method is used the equipment is custom made for the purpose and it is not possible to accidentally behead a volunteer with it. That's good news – that would surely be a career ending performance, decapitating one half of Britain's favourite presenting duo live on television.

Neils Harder – Semi Final

www.youtube.com/watch?v=nB4HMPlmzus

Assuming, incorrectly, that the joke hasn't worn thin yet, Neils Harder burst onto the stage accompanied by backing singers, hunky male dancers and a trio of extremely weak off-the-counter tricks from the magician's catalogue. For the first trick, the Head Twister illusion is a pretty neat effect, but this bulky contraption looks like a typical magician's prop. The magician stands under the device and puts their head into the box from underneath. The box is rotated and it appears that the magician's head is twisting a full three sixty degrees like an owl.

The effect is as simple as they come to perform, relying on space inside the box for the magician to turn their head in the opposite direction once obscured from view. The magician keeps their face visible through a hole in the front of the box and as they start to rotate the box to the right, they turn their head also to the right. When the hole is out of the view of the audience the magician continues to turn the box but rotates their head to the left, awaiting the arrival of the hole on the left side. As the hole lines up with the face the magician rotates their head to the right and it appears that their head, along with the box, rotated a full turn. A nice touch is the little tuft of fake hair on the back of the box that sells the idea that you are looking at the back of the magician's head. They continue rotating the box until the audience has had enough.

As a demonstration of magical thinking I refer to the wonderful magic of Las Vegas magician, Mac King. In his afternoon show in the Harrah's casino that I was lucky enough to catch in 2002, Mac did this same trick in a unique way. Announcing that he had in his possession the "McDonald's Paper Bags of Doom!" he produced two of the brown paper bags that the audience is more used to seeing hamburgers served in. The bags appeared to be the largest and second largest that McDonald's used at the time to package their food and when the bags were fully unfolded one fit neatly inside the other. Mac had cut a hole in the front of both bags and when placing both over his head you could see there was plenty of scope to perform the same effect. By holding the outer bag still with his hand and rotating the inner bag with his other hand the same head-twisting effect was performed in a much more interesting way. Another great learning experience for any magician - Mac King is a brilliantly inventive magician and by thinking outside the box he created a hilarious and fun version of the same effect.

Niels continues his act by opening up a thick hardback book called "Hair Tips" which catches fire and he slams the book shut to extinguish the flames. This seems totally out of context and looks like the magician is simply demonstrating a prop he owns. I would have liked to have seen the fire used to set up the next effect, or for books to be a central part of the next section of the show. Without context, it just appears to be a book that catches fire for no reason. The method for the fire book is much the same as the fire wallet referred to in the explanation of escapology in series three. The book is specially made for the effect and instead of pages it holds a secret, usually a thick strip of fireproof gauze. This gauze is lightly soaked with lighter fluid. As the gauze absorbs the flammable liquid the fluid begins to evaporate, causing flammable vapours to enter the air. Next to the strip is a flint mechanism similar to those found in cigarette lighters. As the book is opened the magician strikes the flint in the mechanism to create a spark which ignites the vapour, causing the illusion of a bonfire in the pages of the ordinary looking book. Again, even as a professional magic prop, these devices can be dangerous in the wrong hands and these tricks should only be attempted by professionals.

A few years ago I was impressed at by a magic dealer who could apparently light a cigarette with his thumb which could catch fire at will. I bought the magic prop from him and examined it later that evening. It was a small flesh coloured pot filled with cotton wool that was designed to be hidden in the hand. A spring loaded lid sealed tightly shut to prevent leaks of lighter fluid that was used to soak the cotton wool. The unit had a flint mechanism attached to create a spark and was attached to an elastic reel, the other end of which attached to the inside of the performer's jacket. The method of the trick was to hold the pot in the fist; then when required flip open the lid, dab the thumb into the soaked cotton wool, then to pull up the thumb while sliding the flint. The idea was the thumb would be lightly covered with the fluid, the spark would light the vapours around the thumb, the magician would hold their thumb aloft and offer a light, then within only a few seconds extinguish the flame by smothering the thumb with the other hand.

I tried to perform this effect in the same way it was demonstrated to me and my thumb didn't light every time. I added more fluid to the cotton wool and tried again. It still didn't work, so with my knowledge that it's the vapours that catch fire and thumb itself does not burn I thought I was safe and put more fluid in – too much.

As I flicked the flint, the spark ignited my thumb just as excess fluid dripped down towards my palm. The flame engulfed my hand as I panicked. As if to add further excitement, the device in my hand caught fire and all I could think to do was to throw it into my back garden. I then ran into the kitchen and extinguished my hand under the tap. The following day I was travelling to Amsterdam to perform magic and ended up spending the whole trip with the hand covered completely in burn plasters and bandages. I tell this story here to reinforce that dangerous magic should never be tried at home. Also, remember that flammable and inflammable mean the same thing. I found that out the hard way too – but that's another story.

Simon buzzed during this part of the performance and I agreed with him. The joke was wearing thin – the combination of being a bit funny, a bit magic and a bit camp wasn't adding up to become something bigger than the sum of its parts and I wondered if the time constraints of a live talent show were contributing to the exhausting, in-your-face performance.

For the final effect, Declan was invited onto the stage and he ended up placed into a contraption which appeared to be full of spikes. The box was closed and the spikes were pushed down by Niels, apparently impaling the other half of the much loved duo, after Neils had done a similar effect to Ant in the previous performance. After Doctor Gore's electric carving knife in series one and the guillotine used by Niels in the previous series there isn't much to be said of this illusion. Once again there are duplicate spikes hidden within the thickness of the table and the spikes that would appear to spear Declan are mechanically stopped above the lovable Geordie so as not to cause injury. Being a magician and having studied magic for many years it is very difficult to watch magic through the eyes of the layperson audience. I imagine that the audience see the magician wheel another big silver box on stage and start rolling their eyes, because we've seen it all before, even within the same series of Britain's Got Talent! However, the audience did seem to enjoy the show, and Niels got a good reaction. It wasn't enough to get his through to the final on this occasion, although as we will see, series eleven was a fantastic year for magic, with three acts in the final.

Matt Edwards – Audition

www.youtube.com/watch?v=iLaCHhkLTGY

Cheeky, lovable, hilarious and incredibly hard working, Matt Edwards arrived on stage as the last act of the day of auditions. The judges appear tired and unexcited but Matt re-energized the room with a hilarious routine with the simplest trick. It reminded me of the scene from the movie Austin Powers where the lead character is unfrozen after thirty years and needs to pee. Austin stands at the urinal and pees for so long that the scene becomes comedy torture and stops being funny, but continues for so long that it becomes funny a second time. You end up laughing again, then laughing it yourself for laughing.

Matt creates his own comedy torture by spilling salt from his hand that just keeps on coming and never seems to stop. Matt has short sleeves so it appears that there is nowhere to hide any device that could be producing the salt and it just keeps appearing like magic! However, as with all the best performers the trick takes second place to the presentation and Matt is hilarious, acting as if he has no idea where it's coming from or how he can stop it. As he slides on the floor the audience and judges find themselves helpless with laughter. This is a great example of the art of comedy magic.

So where is the salt coming from?

A classic of magic, the false thumb tip has been used to conceal silk handkerchiefs, cigarettes, and anything else that can be packed small. The thing I love about the thumb tip is that when you know where to look it appears quite obvious and fake, but the effect in motion is really impressive. The fake thumb is slipped over the real thumb and even if the fake is quite big it still isn't easy to spot when kept moving. The magician holds up their other fist and pushes a space inside by using the fingers and thumbs of the hand with the fake thumb. The last movement in this process is to slip the thumb tip off and leave it inside the fist. The magician then pours the salt, or stuffs the hanky, or extinguishes their cigarette inside the fist. The magician gives the impression that they are tightly packing the contents into the fist by pushing their fingers and thumb of the other hand alternately into the fist. The last push involves the magician stuffing their thumb back into the fake thumb, removing the hand whilst keeping their fist in position. The audience believes the fist is still full of salt but the reality is that the salt is in the fake thumb on the other hand. When the fist is opened to show the salt has disappeared the process is then reversed to reinsert the thumb into the fist so the salt can be poured out.

But how does so much salt get poured back out? In this situation the thumb tip would have to be far too large to get away with. Instead, a specially designed gimmick is used. My guess is that it is the "Salt Pour" gimmick by Tony Clark, available from magic dealers. There are demonstration videos of this that can be seen on the Penguin Magic website that show the gimmick. The process seems much the same as the thumb tip but with a much bigger reservoir for the salt to come from. Also the package that can be purchased comes with everything you need to duplicate the effect. However, there are many illusions and other dealers have similar products. Again, this is a classic piece of magic, but Matt performs it beautifully, and it is hilarious to watch. The judges thought so too, but it was Ant and Dec that enjoyed the act the most, running onto the stage to choose Matt as their golden buzzer winner, giving him a guaranteed place in the semi finals.

Matt Edwards – Semi Final

www.youtube.com/watch?v=v8YlRRtBh2o

After a brilliantly funny entrance, Matt gives yet another great demonstration of magical thinking with a brilliant application of a very simple trick. Two silver balls are used – one is solid and heavy whilst the other is rubber and bouncy. This trick usually involves the magician secretly switching the balls so that the audience volunteer cannot bounce the ball even though the magician can. No-one knows there is more than one ball in play so the magician looks like they are the only one that can make the solid ball bounce. Matt takes this trick and adapts the presentation so that the ball becomes a "sexy detector!" He gets a big laugh as Ant fails to make the ball bounce by saying "I should have used Dec" as a throwaway comment. This trick is often used by magicians who specialise in magic for children as the bouncy ball is a kids toy , but by presenting it in this way Matt gets the adult audience involved and again the focus is on the laughter and comedy, not the simple magic trick.

For the next trick, Ant is given a dice which is rolled to reveal a number that corresponds to a row of numbered cards. Ant is told that he will receive a prize in the form of something that Matt will do to him, based on the number selected. Ant rolls a five, and the card is shown to reveal that Ant has won a hug from Matt. However the audience sees that all the other numbers suggested that Matt was going to kill Ant! Suddenly, a ten-tonne weight drops from the ceiling where Ant was standing.

The easiest way to do this would be to switch the dice to one that has a five on every side, and I suggest this is the method used. Other approaches could be to have a dice that is magnetic on one side and a cup with a magnetic base, which would mean that by shaking the dice and looking inside the cup (which is what most people would do) the dice would always show a five. Or the dice could be weighted to always roll a five. The reason I suggest the first method is that Ant, despite being handed a dice shaker with no table to roll the dice out on, still rolls the dice out of the cup into his other hand, where he looks at it to see the number. This is not what I would expect someone to do – instinctively you would look in the cup. The dice roll in this example seems completely fair, and therefore we have to assume that the dice shows a five on each side. Nothing can be allowed to go wrong in a live TV magic performance and this approach is foolproof – especially as you can be sure that even if Ant did notice that all the sides of the dice were the same he would surely not call out and spoil the show.

Matt Edwards – Final

www.youtube.com/watch?v=JF0P9u55t2I

For Matt's final performance, Dec is given a handful of slips of paper, pens and a cardboard box. Audience members are asked to write the name of a celebrity on each slip of paper. When the box is full, David Walliams is asked to remove one slip of paper and Matt will attempt to read the mind of the judge to identify the randomly chosen celebrity that was chosen by one of the audience members.

Matt then uses what appears to be a hot stick of metal to burn away the edges of a piece of paper on an easel, making holes in the paper, whilst simultaneously mind reading to work out who the celebrity is. When the paper has been sufficiently burned, David is asked to reveal for the first time which celebrity was written – it's Ant and Dec and Matt shows that his artwork is clearly a burned out image of both Ant and Dec. This goes down a storm with the crowd.

There are two main points here. With so many celebrity names to choose from, anything could have been written by the audience members. If ten audience members were chosen at random, that's ten names that went into the box. What would happen if the audience member chose a celebrity that Matt had never heard of? How can Matt be sure that he will be able to create an image of someone that is named by a random member of the audience? As well as this, how can such a detailed piece of artwork be produced so quickly? The answer lies in a brilliant application of the "card force" we looked at earlier. Instead of forcing a choice of a playing card, Matt needs to force the choice of a celebrity, to ensure that no matter who is picked from the audience, and no matter which celebrities they choose, and no matter which piece of paper is chosen by David, the chosen celebrity and image drawn will be Ant and Dec.

The superb magician Mark Shortland created a solution for this that is a masterpiece of engineering and origami. Known as Amazebox and available from magic dealers, the effect is that an ordinary box constructed from folded paper can be used to switch the written celebrity names from one list to another. I recommend the Amazebox as an excellent magical prop and it is well worth the money asked. For this effect, ten audience volunteers write the names of their celebrities on the pieces of paper that are placed inside the box through the slot on the top. When the box is opened there are ten slips of paper for David to choose from but these are not the same slips of paper. The original slips are hidden away and David gets the completely free choice of any of the pieces he sees, which all have the same celebrity written on.

When I perform a similar trick I used to use a gimmicked envelope before I bought an Amazebox. Although the Amazebox is a million times better you can create the same effect by taking two A4 sized brown envelopes with self seal adhesive strips and modifying them to create one gimmicked envelope. It's easy to cut one wall of one envelope out, trim it to make it just a tiny amount smaller and then place it inside the other envelope. The cut out wall forms a flap inside the other envelope, stuck down at the bottom end by the sticky adhesive strip. This leaves you with what appears to be a normal envelope, but with two separate sections within. You can place ten slips of paper all with the same thing written on in one half, then slide the flap over to have what appears to be an empty envelope. Then you start the show, ask volunteers to write on slips of paper and put them in the "empty" envelope. After collecting all the papers, the magician slides the flap across and asks a different volunteer to remove one slip of paper which is coming from the hidden section. Since all these slips were written by the magician earlier, the mind reading effect is easy. To make the envelope more convincing, a strip of the repositionable glue (The "Zig Brand 2 way glue", or blue-glue mentioned earlier) can be applied to the open end of the envelope that the audience put their slips of paper into. As the magician switches to the other side of the envelope the flap becomes glued down, locking away the audience slips from prying eyes.

Even though we know the Ant and Dec image is forced, how do you burn a piece of paper to create the image that is instantly recognisable as Ant and Dec? One way would be to pre-prepare the paper with a flammable image that burns away when contact is made with the hot drawing implement. We never see the drawing being created with only glimpses as Matt turns to face the audience. The majority of the time that Matt creates the artwork the page is obscured as he comically wiggles his backside. I would suggest that the paper is pre-printed with the image of Ant and Dec using a material that burns away as the image is very detailed and clear. If Matt really is an incredible artist skill then he's doing it the hard way.

I thoroughly enjoyed Matt's performances throughout Britain's Got Talent, and I am sure we will see a lot more of him after such great exposure on the show.

DNA – Audition

www.youtube.com/watch?v=gjoNgX2B7pw

DNA arrived on Britain's Got Talent ready to perform a type of magical presentation that had not been seen on the show before. Whilst other acts had done elements of mind reading, DNA devoted their entire presentation to this with an act of mentalism the like of which is most associated with Derren Brown. There's a lot to cover here and some very well presented magic, but there's a risk with mentalism that the performers make the routine too clever and the audience can struggle to follow what's happening. Working on a routine can take months, even years and as performers we get very close to what we are doing. It's difficult to view the act as a non-magician would, and I've seen mind reading and mentalism by world class performers that I've been impressed by as a magician myself but has left friends cold. It's like in traditional magic if the magician makes his assistant disappear from one box and reappear in another – the trick only works if the audience know where the assistant is supposed to be, and adding extra elements to the trick risks confusing matters. When DNA's were creating their performances for Britain's Got Talent I feel there should have been more focus on the audience probably having never seen mentalism before, because some of these routines become quite complicated and I wondered if the audience was following what was happening or tuning out.

For the audition, DNA (Darren 'n Andrew) split up with Darren standing behind Amanda as Andrew took centre stage. Darren asked Amanda to look up one of the contacts on her phone and remember the last three digits of that contacts number. When Amanda has this information in her head, Andrew makes out that he is reading Amanda's mind as he writes on his pad the digits she is thinking of and the name of the contact, Amanda's sister, Debbie.

For the next effect, Simon is asked onto the stage, and handed a pen and pad. Simon is given a free choice of a number, a colour and a celebrity name. Simon writes these on the pad, and Andrew manages to read Simon's mind and names all three things that Simon wrote.

Finally, DNA explain that they started the show wearing camouflage shirts but are both now wearing black shirts.

There are many ways in which these effects can be achieved. For example, Labco Magic is a dealer that specialises in mentalism products. These are often incredible pieces of technology that look like ordinary objects. Their clipboard is incredible, transmitting the image of anything that is drawn on it to a nearby iPad, phone or even smart watch. Their website hides their products behind a question that only magicians would know the answer to, but a quick Google Reverse Image Search is enough to find you the answer to the question if you want to have a browse.

Technology and quality products like these can make it easy to see what is written on a pad even from a distance away. However my favourite device for mentalism is known as the

"Thumper" and I believe this is what is being used to perform this act, at least the first part with Amanda.

The Thumper allows the pair of magicians to communicate secretly with each other using any code the performers choose to be suitable. When activated by one of the magicians, the device sends a signal to a receiver that is hidden from view on the other magician's body – usually attached to an arm covered by a sleeve, or leg covered by the trouser. Upon activating the Thumper makes a hard tap against the magician's arm or leg. This can be used to transmit the thought of numbers from one magician to the other very easily by simply pressing the activator as many times as needed for each digit. To take the use of this item further, morse-code can be used to transmit letters. During the presentation of the effect, DNA reveal the numbers first leaving a space for the audience to applaud, allowing time for the transmission of the name of the contact.

With the available technology there are many ways that minds can be read, but there are not as many ways to reveal that information to the audience. Often I feel that the secret is more interesting than the effect because mentalism tends to end up looking much the same as this performance, whoever does it. Every routine seems to end up with the magician holding a pad, showing he's written the words you were thinking off, and there are many mentalists who perform acts that are sometimes indistinguishable from one another. For the best mentalism routines I am aware of I would have no hesitation in recommending Derren Brown's live theatre shows, many of which are available on DVD. Again, I'd love to be able to watch mentalism as a layperson, to see how it feels to be fooled, but once you know the methods used it's down to the performance and showmanship to make it stand out, and mentalism is difficult to build into something greater because it all boils down to the big reveal of thoughts written on a pad.

The judges were all impressed and DNA made it to the next round.

DNA – Semi Final

www.youtube.com/watch?v=VnFD6WlYexY

For the next round, DNA presented more mentalism with a routine that I really enjoyed. Walking onto the stage with a dictionary, in hand, David Walliams was invited to think of a word, and this was a genuine free choice of word. David writes the word on a pad handed to him by a stagehand. Meanwhile, Darren approaches the judges with a deck of cards. Darren separates the cards into piles and randomly shuffles the first pile in front of Simon. Simon says "stop" and the top card is placed on the table, and the rest of the pile is placed in Darren's pocket. The same process is repeated twice more so each of the three judges has a selected card.

The educated magician (and that includes you if you have read this far) again spots the unusual nature of the card selection – why not just allow the judges to name a card each? Or fan the cards and ask them to select one. Something funny is going on.

The three cards are mixed and randomly distributed between the three judges. This is truly random and the mechanics of the trick will need to take this into account.

Andrew on stage takes a pack from his pocket and removes three cards. He then successfully explains that he knows all the three cards that the judges would choose. Not only this, but the cards were the ones the judges were destined to pick all along, as Andrew's cards have the judges names written on them, with each judges name printed on the card they chose.

Finally, DNA reminds us that at the beginning of the performance David Walliams chose a word randomly in his mind. They take a pad from off-stage and Darren writes onto the pad. We expect to see the word David was thinking of, but Darren writes "1414R11". What could this mean? Of course, the dictionary – it's been there with Simon for the whole time, and Simon is requested to turn to page 1414, look in the right hand column and look at the eleventh word. Sure enough, the word at that location in the dictionary is the same word that David was thinking of.

The temptation to increase the power of a mentalism routine by adding more content and coincidence can turn off an audience that loses track of what is supposed to be happening and we almost see this in DNA's routine. Simon is obviously not expecting to have to look through the dictionary and does not have his glasses on. The sudden request to quickly find a specific word in a massive dictionary flummoxes the judges and it would have been easy for them to make a mistake in the counting and read the wrong word. Luckily it all works out, but the trick ends in almost chaos and would have been just as good without that last part anyway. Perhaps as a learning experience the dictionary could have been handed to the judges with the instruction that they would need to look up a word later, and the judges would have been able to make sure the book was passes to someone with good eyesight.

To explain this routine we need to look closely at what's happening, reverse engineer the effects and work on the basis that it's not possible to actually read minds. This makes it a lot simpler, especially as we now know about devices such as the Thumper that can transmit information from one magician to the other. Darren performs a neat force, which I suspect uses a deck treated with an effect we've seen before on the show – the old Rough and Smooth fluid.

When Darren removes the deck from pack, I believe this is a rough and smooth forcing deck where the cards are in pairs. As we've already seen with the Invisible Deck performed by Jamie Raven, the roughing fluid makes the treated card stick to another card with the same fluid treatment. This means that the pack of cards handles with every pair of cards sticking together as if they are only one card, when the magician applies a little pressure to the pairs of cards. When the cards are handled loosely the pairs separate. For this effect, I believe that the deck is divided into thirds. The three force cards are duplicated across a third of the deck each. This means that the top third of the deck consists of pairs, each card in the pair is face down, and the top card of each pair is the five of spades. The next third of the deck is the same but with a different top card (nine of diamonds is the top card in each pair) and the third section has the two of hearts as the top card in each pair. With all the cards facing down and each pair sticking together because of the roughing fluid, the pack can be turned face up to show a whole pack of different cards.

The cards are divided into three piles, one for each judge. This means that each pile consists of cards in pairs, with the top card of each pair the same as all the other top cards in the pile.

When the magician mixes the cards, he is moving pairs from the top to the bottom of the piles which handle as if only one card. This means that whenever Simon says "stop" the top card will always be the first force card. When the other judges say "stop" they too will get their force cards. With the three "random" cards selected it's apparent that using this method the three cards will be the cards the magician chose to use – not a free choice at all.

To add more randomness, the cards are distributed between the three judges by an ad-hoc selection. This genuine mix is countered by the on-stage performer who has all his options covered as we will see later. The three cards that were selected by the judges are currently in a preset order, so when they are randomly handed to the judges through a choice of "top, middle or bottom), the on-stage performer knows which judge got which card. He can remove a deck from his pocket and look through to locate the chosen cards. Within that deck there are three of each of the possible force cards, (that's three fives of spades, three nines of diamonds and three twos of hearts). This means that, knowing that Simon got the five of spades the magician simply removes the five of spades that says Simon and ignores the other two five of spades that say Alicia and Amanda on. He removes the nine of diamonds with Amanda's name on and the two of hearts with Alicia's name on.

Finally, the two magicians on stage ask David to think of his word from earlier. David still has the piece of paper with the word on in his pocket. He does not have one important thing – the clipboard that the pad was attached to, or the pad that he wrote on. The secret here could be a special clipboard from a company like Labco Magic, or could be something as simple as a piece of carbon paper on the clipboard. Whichever method is used, the stagehand who takes the clipboard back from David Walliams gets sight of the chosen word, and immediately looks this up offstage in the dictionary. What I would do if I was performing this trick would be to have the stagehand write the exact information I need (the page number, column and word location) in the same format that I will write it a moment later, on the pad in light pencil, so I can copy it in thick marker for the audience. This ties in with what we see in this performance as the pad is off-stage and the magician goes over to get it from behind the curtain. The stagehand could write somewhere off-stage the information required and this could be glimpsed when the pad is collected from the side of the stage by the magician, but I believe this approach is too prone to error. Should the magician forget what they saw they would need to go back for another look. It's far better to write the information lightly on the pad, so the magician can copy it in thick marker pen, removing any margin of error. Or perhaps, if the magician would like to hand the pad out to the audience for inspection afterwards, why not have the stagehand write the information on a sticky label and attach it to the pen? No-one is looking too closely at pen and this could be put in an inside pocket after the information has been written, leaving the magician totally clean. Either way, it's a lovely routine and even with the complicated ending which seems to confuse the judges, it goes down really well and the audience agree – DNA makes it to the final!

DNA - Final

www.youtube.com/watch?v=opD63UUTRms

One of the major issues that faces magicians on television is the audience's favourite question – "what are you going to do next week?"

I saw a documentary from the 1970s about the world of cabaret where acts discussed the impact of television on their working lives. Comedians, magicians and other variety acts would spend their careers performing the same routines over and over again as they toured around the country. A gig in a working-men's-club was an opportunity to show your act whilst also learning what went well and where the show could be improved upon. Over the years, performing night after night, the performance would become a highly polished piece of work and by the time the whole of the country had been covered the audience would have forgotten what they had seen and the act could be toured again. Many performers of that era refer to "squandering an act" by showing it on television. The audience says, sure, that was really good, wonder what they will do next week? TV churns up and spits out an act in one five minute window that may have been successful on the club circuit for years.

For magicians the only option is to continue making something bigger and better than the previous performance. The need to keep innovating and coming up with new fresh ideas is a real challenge in magic. You can see from the number of examples in this book how we have seen the same methods producing completely different effects, but in mind reading and mentalism it can be a challenge to keep presenting the act in new and novel ways. In my opinion, DNA's final act upped the energy, added more content and upped the complexity but ultimately it lost me completely. By the end I had no idea what was supposed to be happening or what had just happened. Simon agreed in his comments after the performance.

The YouTube video is titled "DNA Blow Our Minds with Numbers" and I think this effect totally blew the minds of everyone watching and not in the way DNA would have wanted. The whole act appeared an increasingly baffling mess.

An overly complicated method is used to generate a random number. This involves a calculator on a Smartphone being used to multiply freely chosen numbers together. The end result is the number 27204141 – apparently completely randomly arrived at. This is not the case – there are magician's apps for smart-phones that look like the stock calculator that comes with the phone, but can be programmed to show whatever answer the magician chooses when the "=" key is pressed.

Another method can be performed with any scientific calculator by typing in the answer you need followed by a short code. To use the example above, take your scientific calculator and type 27204141, followed by the plus key, then zero, then the multiply key, then the open bracket key. This leaves the calculator displaying zero and looking unprepared, and you can enter any mathematical calculation you wish from this point. When you press the equals key the display will show 27204141.

David Walliams is then asked to choose a word from a random location in one of his books. This throws in the first potential confusion in the audience's mind as this is nothing to do with the calculator trick that we feel we are still in the middle of.

The performance has changed to a different effect entirely, and this is confusing to the flow of the performance.

David chooses a page and a word and Andrew attempts to guess this information by mind reading. We know that he is not reading the judges mind because David does not know the page number, he admits this during the trick, so quite where this information is coming from is anyone's guess. Again, if this was real, there would be no reason to use a book – David could think of a word at random. Even using the book there is no need for the other magician to stand with him helping him choose the page and the word. The word that David was thinking of was "Lady", but the word I'm thinking of was "Thumper" because the magician is standing over David's shoulder the whole time, looking at the chosen word, which should not be necessary because it's the other magician doing the mind reading – so they must be signalling to each other.

The magicians take back to the stage for the finale which is one of the most confusing things I have ever seen in magic. DNA reminds us that the number that was "randomly" reached earlier using the trick calculator was 27204141. They explain that in the previous performance the page number in the dictionary was 1414, and as you can clearly see, the last four digits of the number tonight are 1414. For me this was baffling as the numbers as read from left to right are 4141. The confusion continues – we are told that four judges made the decisions, and a four is added to the whiteboard on stage. The number in the telephone trick in the audition was 415 and this is also written on the board. Simon chose the number 717 in the audition. Those numbers when added together (4, 4, 1, 5, 7, 1, 7) add up to 29.

Are you still following this?

These numbers are written on the board underneath the previous number. The magicians now show that the first half of the randomly calculated number (2720 or 2, 7 and 20) also add up to 29.

I believe that this is meant to be impressive, but it's been so hard to follow up to this point that we're just taking their word for it that it adds up. In the overall trick the fact that both numbers add up to 29 is a complete red herring anyway, and such a distraction that it overcomplicates the finale which keeps going with yet more reveals.

Now, we are shown that if the original number is divided up differently it can be displayed as 2,7,20,4,14,1. What?

Then, if you assign a letter of the alphabet to each number with A=1 and B=2, then these letters spell out BGTDNA which is the name of the show and the name of the act. Even knowing the secrets I was utterly baffled as I had no idea what was going on, where I was and my why head was hurting. Even the performer on stage said that Simon was looking confused and he wasn't the only one. DNA were the lowest scoring act in the final and it was a shame to see them bomb so badly – they did a great job throughout the series but by adding that extra layer the final act it took me a couple of extra viewings before I knew what was supposed to be happening, and I doubt the BGT audience had a clue. A massive learning experience for any magician – when you practice your act over and over so meticulously you get too close to it and you should take a step back, stop and try to see your act as a fresh pair of eyes would.

Issy Simpson – Audition

www.youtube.com/watch?v=gSYa6_Siivs

Issy Simpson appeared on Britain's Got Talent at the age of eight years old. In her audition, Issy explained that her Granddad teaches her magic. If the high standard of her magic is above and beyond our expectations then there is a reason for this. Issy's Granddad is a man named Russ Stevens, who has worked as professional magician for many years and is an expert in the craft. He has also worked as a magical advisor in

Britain's Got Talent. Issy got a lot of stick in the press for this, with many accusing her of cheating. Whilst it's true that many of the effects Issy performed on the show were achieved with self-working, expensive props, Issy still managed to make the performance endearing to the audience, and at the risk of sounding like a stuck record, the secret is the smallest part of the magic show, and winning the audience over with showmanship and personality is the key. Sure, anyone could operate these tricks, but could they perform them – to a crowd of thousands, a live TV audience of millions? Issy did a great job.

For the audition, Issy walked over to the judges holding a cardboard box full of books. Each book is examined by a judge, with David Walliams being given a copy of his own book, The Midnight Gang. Issy asks Simon to put the cardboard box on the floor but Simon finds he is not strong enough to lift it. Even with David Walliams' help they cannot lift it. Issy goes back to the box and removes a deck of cards from inside, then casually lifts the box up and takes it back to the stage. Issy appears to be stronger than two grown men! This is the first of Issy's expensive props – the box has a suction mechanism built into the base that the magician can activate at will. The box is self working but we don't care because the effect is hilarious and Issy delivers the performance with a sense of mischief and fun.

Simon is asked to choose a card from the deck and here we see another use of the Rough and Smooth deck. This time, I suspect every card in each pair to be a seven of diamonds on the top, allowing Issy to show the cards are all different underneath, but forcing Simon to take the card that matches the one to be revealed later.

Alicia is asked to choose a random word from a random page from the random book. This time Issy heads back to the stage where another magician's prop is waiting. The blackboard looks a lot like one that was featured in the FISM magic convention in 2015 by a company called Lynx Magic. The Lynx Blackboard allows a free choice of word and a magician can make the chosen word appear on the blackboard. The promotional video on YouTube by magic dealer MagicTao, explains everything, which surprises me how much depth it goes into. The blackboard contains the mechanism familiar to users of computer plotters, drawing on the blackboard in chalk. The blackboard connects to an off-stage assistant using a phone or tablet computer to draw what they want to appear on the blackboard. The plotter mechanism copies the image drawn on the tablet and then drops out of sight inside the frame of the whiteboard. I would not normally reveal a secret such as this but as this information is freely available online (it's the first search result on Google when you search by the name of the product), so it's information that is in the public domain already.

Finally, Issy reveals that she is wearing a hidden T-Shirt with Simon holding the forced card printed on. This extra bit of magic sealed the deal – Issy sailed through to the semi final.

Issy Simpson – Semi Final

www.youtube.com/watch?v=IWT59QO7DhQ

For the next trick, Issy pulled out another large scale illusion (have you seen the price of the blackboard from the previous trick?) and we see another use of the magic chair that was used by both Brynolf and Ljung, and Darcy Oake in previous series. The adult assistant disappears under the curtain and Issy comes out of the hidden compartment.

Issy showed the judges that there was an envelope high up above the stage, far out of reach of anyone wishing to tamper with it. She has written a letter, sealed inside the envelope and heads down to talk to the judges.

Issy asks Alicia to take a piece of paper from a transparent bag filled with slips of paper, each with a different number written down. Fans of Brynolf and Ljung may remember this bag being filled with DVD's during the semi final of series six. Just as they used it to force the choice of a specific DVD, Issy uses it to force Alicia to choose a specific number.

Simon Cowell is asked to name someone famous. Simon chooses himself.

Amanda is asked to choose a specific time of day to the hour and minute.

David is asked to take the change from his pocket and count it. In doing so, Issy now has three random answers. The celebrity is Simon Cowell, the favourite time of day is 6.30pm and amount of change in David Walliam's pocket was £2.01p.

Issy then goes up onto the stage and takes down the envelope (having to stand on a chair to do so, she's only eight!). Inside the envelope is revealed to be a letter about her day in London. Within the letter it mentions that she went to Madame Tussaud's and saw Simon Cowell (prediction one), then she saw the time on Big Ben was 6.30pm (prediction two) and her granddad bought her an Ice cream (which was £2.01p, a lot less than this trick cost, I'll bet!).

Finally Alicia reads out the number she chose at random, which appears to be another prediction achieved, although this number was forced using the force bag to make it match the date of the performance, adding a little extra flourish to a really nicely performed show.

We know that Alicia's number was forced, but how did Issy know to write the other three predictions before the show began? The envelope was there the whole time and clearly visible before any of the judges had given any of their answers. The secret lies in the chair that was briefly wheeled onto the stage so that Issy could collect the envelope. Offstage, an assistant is listening to the judges' answers and filling in the gaps in the letter that was written before the show. As soon as the assistant has filled in the name of the celebrity, the amount of money and the favourite time of day, the letter is folded up and loaded into a special compartment on the back of the chair. The chair is taken onto the stage and Issy climbs up. She retrieves the envelope hanging from the rafters and secretly loads the hidden letter from the back of the chair to the back of the envelope. You can see on the broadcast that after climbing down from the chair she pushes it backwards a little and loads the envelope at the same time. All that remains is for her to read the letter to the crowd to rapturous applause. Again, this is a shop bought trick and probably out of the reach of many eight year olds with their pocket money, but it's the way that the trick is performed that makes it heart-warming and the audience loved it. Issy won the public vote and headed to the final.

Issy Simpson – Final

www.youtube.com/watch?v=y4bMcxN6rdY

Issy dedicates her final performance (and the final magic performance of the series to date) to her brother Dexter. Issy heads towards the judges and takes out a pack of cards which has a word or name on the back of each card. We see the words that Issy has chosen reflect things from her life. Walliams (Issy's favourite Judge), snow (she loves snow!) and so on. Simon is given a free choice of card and Issy looks through the pack to find that card. As she does this, Issy explains she knows that specific card would have been Simon's choice and it's so strange that he chose the card that she also called Simon. The card is removed from the deck then placed on the bottom. I believe the bottom card of the deck already had "Simon" written on the back, and a dab of our old favourite, "Zig 2-Way Glue" on the face. By placing the chosen card on the bottom of the deck it sticks to the card above it and the magic move is completed – the chosen card now appears to say Simon on the back, because it's really two cards stuck together. This is yet another application of repositionable blue-glue we've seen in this book and it's a brilliant tool for magicians.

Finally, Issy takes a blank card and rips it up into pieces, then heads out in the audience to join her brother Dexter. Issy mentioned that they love to play in the snow and Issy makes a snowstorm appear from the chair that Dexter is sat in. This again is a purpose made stage illusion and creates the effect that it is snowing indoors. My favourite demonstration of the Snowstorm Illusion is performed by the magician Kevin James, and with more time to devote to the performance it's absolutely beautiful as the entire theatre is covered in snow apparently from the magician's hands and I'd recommend checking it out.

The Snowstorm Illusion is an incredible effect when seen live on stage. The magician looks to be producing the snow from their hands and they appear alone on stage. The juxtaposition of the solo magician and huge snowing effect is magical and one you remember for a long time. Even though the snow is simply coming from the specially manufactured stool which is loaded with fans and other gimmicks, somehow the audience suspends their disbelief. It's one of my favourite magical effects and it's beautiful in the right hands. For a time limited TV talent show performance, Issy did a great job, but this effect is an entire act on its own and really needs the time for the scene to be set, the story to be unfolded and finally, the snow to fall down over the audience.

Matt, DNA and Issy did a fantastic job in showing that magic is a great branch of the performing arts, that it's never too young to start learning, and that a great performance can get you a long way. Whilst none of them became the overall series winner, Series 11 was still the most successful of all the series for magic yet.

Afterword: The Masked Magician.

Well – that's the end of the book. But there's just one more thing I'd like to share with you.

When I was a kid, there was a TV show called, "Magician's Secrets Revealed". This started as a one-off TV Special that purported to reveal magicians closely guarded secrets. The show was very popular and spawned a series, with many tricks being revealed in every episode, including a fair amount that actually went on to appear in Britain's Got Talent episodes all those years later. Initially, magicians were furious about this programme because they don't want people to know how the tricks are done. People proclaimed that the Masked Magician was destroying the art of magic by explaining the methods. Looking back on this period, the show actually seemed to have done some good. It didn't kill off the art of magic, but I know of many people who found this show fascinating and developed an interest in magic themselves. Knowing some of the secrets is a great way to get involved, and maybe one day become a performer yourself – I know I did. I really enjoyed the Masked Magician programmes, but there was one thing that used to really annoy me about them, and I'll try to put that into words here.

The shows narrator often had a sneering approach to the performance. When the trick was revealed, he'd often say something like, "and now you know the secret. Huh. Not very magical, is it?" This is not the approach I think the show should have taken. With hindsight, the Masked Magician tended to reveal big stage illusions, the kind that dominated Britain's Got Talent in the early series.

The masked magician showed us that the girl slid into a secret compartment, or pulled a hidden lever. Magic allows us to suspend our disbelief whilst we watched the performance, but if we did choose to ponder on how it worked, did we really think she disappeared by magic? Or did we assume a lever was hidden somewhere? The masked magician didn't give away secrets in that sense, he merely confirmed your suspicions if you wondered how it was done.

The Metamorphosis trick described earlier in this book was revealed on one of the Masked Magician shows. The magician is locked in a trunk, and his assistant stands on the top of it. A curtain is raised, and then dropped to reveal that the magician is now standing on the trunk. He unlocks the trunk to find his assistant inside. Metamorphosis became the signature routine for Jonathan and Charlotte Pendragon, who performed this on television many times. Their version of Metamorphosis was flawlessly choreographed every time (almost – there's one hilarious outtake which you may find on YouTube), and the moment where the assistant and magician change places was done in the blink of an eye. It's a good trick but when the Pendragons do it, it's absolutely extraordinary.

When the Masked Magician performed the trick, the method he used was probably the same as that used by the Pendragons but instead of the split second changeover that the Pendragons perfected, the Masked Magician laboured over the switch, lifting the curtain multiple times. Eventually, the Metamorphosis happened, and the magician changed places with the assistant. The trick was explained in detail, and the sneering narrator told us how it's not very magical and now you know the methods.

Some would accept that and believe they know the answer. Not me. The narrator continued to explain magical methods throughout many episodes and often threw in a smart-alec line about how it's not magic at all. But I've seen the Pendragons perform their Metamorphosis many times. It really is magical. Actually, it's one of the greatest pieces of magic I have ever seen. For the Masked Magician to reveal the secret wasn't an issue for me, I wanted to know. But, the TV show presented magic as merely a puzzle to be solved. There was no discussion of the artistry, the performance, the skills of everyone involved to make such a wonderful piece of entertainment. They seemed to believe that once you knew the secret, that was the end of it. Even now, twenty years on, no-one's done Metamorphosis with the speed and artistry of The Pendragons and it remains a classic of magic. As with all magic, it's not what you're doing, it's how you present it.

For me, knowing the secret is the start of your journey into magic. Now you have read the methods that I believe were used by so many performers on Britain's Got Talent, I hope this insight has allowed you to see the importance of the Presentation. Knowing the methods is akin to knowing how Beethoven plays the piano. Sure, he's simply pressing the notes at the right time and in the right order, but can anyone simply take that information and play the piano as well as Beethoven did? Of course not. But what if Beethoven's piano playing inspired you to not only learn to play, but to innovate, to compose, to push boundaries and come up with things no-one has ever done before? That's what I hope is the purpose of this book.

We live in an age where you can find many tricks exposed on the internet. It can be easy to find explanations of where the hidden lever may be hidden, or how the magician lifts two playing cards whilst pretending to lift only one. But it's the practice, the artistry and the performance that separates the tedious pub performer, the bore at the bar and the tacky cruise ship act from the world class performances you see from a Britain's Got Talent finalist or series winner. If you take one thing away from this book, it should be that the best magic doesn't need complex methods and trickery. It needs real magical thinking, showmanship, flair and charisma. Now you know these methods, I hope that you can see clearly that maybe 10% of what you see is the mechanism behind the performance; the other 90% is the performance itself. If you read this book in order to find answers to your puzzles then that's up to you. I hope that as you finish reading, you have a better understanding of the importance of the performance.

Printed in Great Britain
by Amazon